Frome Society for

Drawing: Is…

FROME SCHOOL OF ART.
BUILT 1902 · DEMOLISHED 1997·

1

Stephen and Jeremy Yates, great-grandsons of J W Singer with members of FSLS and guests, at the unveiling of the plaque on 4 November 2019

Photo: Mendip Times

The plaque reads:

Frome Art Metalworks

was established in 1866 by **John Webb Singer** (1819-1904) who became renowned worldwide for his ecclesiastical work and from 1888 for casting in bronze some of our most iconic public statues including Boudica by Westminster Bridge, Justice on the Old Bailey and Oliver Cromwell outside the Houses of Parliament.

After statuary work ceased in 1927, a metal foundry continued on this site until 1999.

Frome Society for Local Study

FOREWORD

Firstly, I would like to thank Sara Morris for agreeing that I write this foreword to the tenth and final Yearbook that I shall have edited. It has been a great pleasure to follow Michael McGarvie who has set such a high standard of which the Frome Society can be proud. The quality of these ten Yearbooks has only been possible owing to the superb design and layouts created by Cliff and Janet Howard, and the late Alan Yeates and I thank them for their flair and expertise. These Yearbooks could only have been collated through the continued interest in the town and local countryside, the history of its buildings and inhabitants and the authors' commitment. Over these ten years, there have been one hundred articles written by members, representing two thirds of all the articles published and there has been a regular increase in the proportion culminating in only two articles written by non-members this year. The quality of the Yearbook has always depended on the articles and photographs submitted and I thank all the authors who have contributed and ask you to continue by helping my successor in the future.

This miscellany covers such a breadth of Frome's history, touching on two world famous artists, a potter and a sculptor, a pupil of Alfred Munnings and a forgotten author subsequently lionised by a Nobel laureate. Three individuals who had a major influence on the town during the 19th century are remembered. There is a delightful description of the discovery of a young woman's collection of family postcards, the research of a family photograph and, as usual, there are descriptions of Frome buildings, their various uses and history, an explanation of the ubiquitous Cockey lamps, and finally there is further ongoing research on the foundation of a mediaeval mill at Spring Gardens and the extraordinary discovery of a Saxon weapon.

As I write this at the end of April, a strange time when we are all locked away from each other, FSLS is unable to function normally; by the time you read this, I hope that we shall all have come through it and regard it as past history that can be recorded in future Yearbooks.

I would like to say a special word of thanks to Pat Eames who has read and corrected the proofs of the Yearbooks and many other FSLS publications over the years, and to give my best wishes to Mick Davis, the new editor.

Alastair MacLeay

3

CONTENTS

Amy Singer and Camille Claudel

by Sue Bucklow

My fascination with Amy Singer began when I started working on the Singers archive of glass negatives twenty years ago. The archive contained a photograph of the Singer family with the famous French sculptor Camille Claudel. I was already a great admirer of Claudel and here in the archive was a photograph of her taken in Frome in 1886. I couldn't quite believe it, but I soon realised that the reason Camille was here in Frome was that she and Amy Singer shared a studio together in Paris. Camille Claudel was here visiting her friend. This immediately piqued my interest and I wanted to find out more about John Webb Singer's daughter and how, in her early twenties, she came to be in Paris training to be a sculptor and became friends with Claudel and Rodin, two of the greatest sculptors of the late 19th and early 20th centuries.

Trying to piece together and tell the story of Amy Singer is more difficult than it would first appear; her correspondence and her own work have disappeared. This may in part be due to the fact that she had no children and thus no immediate family to bequeath it to. But I was fortunate in stumbling across several documents in the archives when researching *Casting the World: The Story of J.W. Singer & Sons, Frome* [1].

I found a definitive photograph of Amy Singer working in her Frome studio on a bust of her father (sadly the whereabouts of this bust is unknown). The photograph was pasted into a scrapbook belonging to her brother Edgar, and annotated by him. It must date from the later 1880s when she had returned from Paris. Having exhibited many times at the recent Royal Academy Summer Exhibitions, she is surrounded by her work. Amy's favoured material appears to have been terracotta and her subjects were men of standing, well known in their fields of expertise. In 1882 she exhibited a bust of General Sir Charles Staveley, Commander of British troops in China and Hong Kong; in 1885 there are two busts, one of Rev George Tugwell, an expert on marine life, and the other is of Samuel Carter Hall, editor of The Art Journal. In 1887, her most prolific year for exhibiting, there were four busts: Rev Whitwell Elwin, who was editor of the Quarterly Review; significantly he was the grandfather of Amy's future husband Fountain Peter Elwin, one of Amy's nieces, Beryl Singer, the daughter of her brother Herbert and the other busts are of Sargeant Charles Fletcher and Rev Arthur Brooking of Bovingdon.

Amy was born in 1862, the third child of John's marriage to his second wife Sarah, née Doswell from Barnstaple. Herbert would then have been eight and Edgar four. They were all living above the Singer business premises at 25 Market Place selling watches, clocks and jewellery. The year before Amy's birth, in the 1861 census, John Webb Singer described himself as a watchmaker, but he was already employing eight men and six boys on metalworking, and had two forges on Justice Lane, supplying candlesticks and other ecclesiastical work to churches throughout the British Isles. It is no wonder that Singer needed to expand and by 1866 he had opened his new works at Waterloo. Amy's childhood coincided with busy times in the Singer household and it must have been a hive of activity;

the works were always expanding. New lines had to be supplied with designs and metal-workers trained to make them.

Amy Singer in her studio working on a portrait bust of her father in the 1880s
Photo: South West Heritage Trust

Amy's father had a great love of art and aesthetics. He opened the Frome Art School in 1865 which had a syllabus based on that taught at the South Kensington Art Schools. He nurtured this love in his children who were lucky enough to be enrolled in London. Herbert, Edgar and Amy all studied at the South Kensington Art Schools, then housed in what is now the Henry Cole Wing of the Victoria and Albert Museum. The Singer household must have been very cosmopolitan: Singer undertook many trips to the continent, making contact with Flemish metal-workers and finding inspiration for new designs. Being able to speak French would have been important and the 1871 census shows the family also had a live-in French teacher, Matilda Poulain which must have helped Amy in future life, after she had completed her studies in London.

One of Amy's tutors at South Kensington was the French sculptor, Jules Dalou. He was a Communard who had fled France after the siege of Paris in 1871, rather than face life imprisonment for his role in the uprising. He had connections to the Académie Colarossi in Paris, which allowed women students access to life studies, a practice unheard of at the Royal Academy in London, where women were banned from the life room. Amy and fellow student, Emily Fawcett, broke free of this constraint and chose the Colarossi, leaving for Paris in the early 1880s.

Here they met and became friends with Camille Claudel, with whom they shared a studio at 117 rue Notre Dame des Champs in the heart of Montparnasse. This street was full with studios of both artists and sculptors, more than any other in Paris at this time, so they found themselves at the very heart of the Bohemian art world. In 1882, already an eminent sculptor, Auguste Rodin became the patron of their studio, and they were joined by another English student, Jessie Lipscomb. Working together meant they could share the rent and the cost of models.

117 rue Notre Dame des Champs, Montparnasse   Photos: Sue Bucklow

The address at rue Notre Dame des Champs still exists; it had a ground floor studio, now an apartment, but with the same entrance and internal courtyard. All the girls were in their early twenties, experiencing a freedom they did not have in London. Thanks to William Elborne, Jessie Lipscomb's boyfriend and a keen amateur photographer, there are several photographs of the interior of the building. These mainly show Camille and Jessie working on sculptures, or sitting around smoking and chatting, but thanks to the Somerset Archives scrapbook photograph of Amy in her studio, I can now identify Amy in one of the Paris photographs which also includes Camille and her brother Paul Claudel.

As their patron, Auguste Rodin was a frequent visitor to the studio as he was responsible for critiquing their work. There is a letter in the archives of the Musée Rodin from John Webb Singer to Rodin, thanking him for the lessons and advice that Amy received. It was written in 1885 the year in which Amy's time in Paris was cut short due to her father suffering a serious illness. She returned to Frome to be with him and her family. Her correspondence with Rodin from this time also survives and it is clear that she was incredibly frustrated by this turn of events. She writes to Rodin: *Merci bien des fois, mon père va un peu mieux. Moi je m'ennuie et je ne fais rien, étant toujours en visite à présent; je devais être partie pour une autre mais je suis enrhumée heureusement-et j'attends le bon moment pour retourner à Paris- et je suis si jalouse de tout le monde qui est là à présent. Je vous envoie, Cher Monsieur, mes amitiés les plus sincères.* She was desperate to get back to her life in Paris with Camille and her fellow studio partners. It must have been hard to be stuck in provincial Frome when she had been living her life at the very heart of the Parisian art world.

Whether Amy was able to return to Paris before Camille's visit to Frome in July 1886 is unclear. Camille arrived with fellow studio partner, Jessie Lipscomb, who may well have been the photographer of the group photo taken outside North Hill Cottage, the Singer

family home.
Camille stayed on after Jessie left, enjoying day trips to Bath and Bristol with the family.

The Singer family with Camille Claudel outside North Hill Cottage, July 1888.
Standing: Camille Claudel, Amy Singer, Edgar Singer. Seated: Sarah and John Webb
Singer with granddaughter Beryl   *Photo: Frome Museum*

She also had a tour of both the Frome Art School and the foundry premises at Waterloo. This was just prior to the casting of large-scale statuary, but Camille would have seen sand casting of smaller pieces and she would probably have also seen the photography studio set up at Singers, and how all goods were photographed prior to despatch. Camille was deeply interested in photography; she and Amy had written to Jessie Lipscomb on a rainy day during her stay asking Jessie to send the glass plate negatives taken of their trip. It appears that Camille also had her portrait taken at Singers and this is one of the glass plate negatives that has survived. It has since been cleaned and printed and is an incredibly detailed portrait.

The photograph of the Paris studio group, including Amy, is dated 1887. Whether this means that Amy returned to Paris to work, or whether she is just visiting is unknown. After Amy was forced to return to England, Rodin had chosen Camille and Jessie to work as assistants in his studio. They both worked on the 'Burghers of Calais' but sometime in 1887 Jessie returned to England after she found it too difficult to work with both Camille and Rodin, who had started their turbulent relationship. Camille's affair with Rodin was to last for eight years, throughout which time her brilliant skills as a sculptor were employed on all his large commissions as well as making her own work. When their relationship ended Camille struggled to survive as an artist in her own right. After a breakdown, her family had Camille committed to Ville-Evrard at Neuilly sur Seine, a mental institution where she remained for over thirty years until her death in 1943. Jessie never forgot her friend and visited her in the asylum in 1929.

We do not know whether Amy also made that pilgrimage, but like Jessie she also kept in touch with Rodin. There is an intriguing letter in the Musée Rodin, which is not dated but must have been written whilst John Webb Singer was still alive. She is writing at her father's behest to enquire whether the Singers Foundry can cast Rodin's work for any exhibition that he might have in either England or Paris and Amy signs it: *Votre élève affectionnée Amy Mary Fountaine -*

Friends at rue Notre Dame des Champs: Amy Singer, Emily Fawcett, Paul Claudel, William Elborne, Camille Claudel

Elwin. Rodin obviously replied and Amy writes back: *Mon cher Monsieur Rodin, merci beaucoup pour votre lettre et je suis trés heureuse de savoir que vous m'avez pas oubliée.* Again it is unknown whether Singers cast any of Rodin's work and whether Amy managed to visit Rodin as she hoped to do, since this is the last piece of correspondence between them in the Musée Rodin archive.

Thanks to the sculptor Hamo Thornycroft, we know that Amy was living in Frome again in 1888, as he lovingly describes the scene at North Hill Cottage in letters he wrote to his wife, during his stay there for two nights on 19 and 20 November. Having been collected from the station by Herbert Singer and arriving at North Hill Cottage, he writes: *soon landed here in a house chock-full of curiosities of art on a small scale, bits of brass and china from every land. Mr and Mrs Singer senior are a nice couple and most hospitable....Miss Singer, a clever cheery girl, is I think sensibly aesthetic and as you know a sculptor. The man she is engaged to is staying in the house, and we had some good stories in the smoking room tonight.* It is interesting to note that Thornycroft and his wife Agatha already know that Amy is a sculptor. In a letter written on the day he is leaving he writes: *The Singers at Frome were most kind and hospitable. Miss S entrusted to me a little bronze for you, she is such a clever interesting girl'* It would be marvellous to know what Amy's bronze was, but to have this kind of description is wonderful; it brings Amy to life.

Probable portrait of Camille Claudel printed from collodion glass plate negative taken during her visit to Frome in 1888   *Photo: Frome Museum*

Amy's fiancé had an unusual name of Fountain Peter Elwin. Amy and he were married at St John's Church, Frome on 19 June 1889, both aged of 27. He was a descendant of John Rolfe and Pocahontas, the American Indian 'princess' who came to England in the late 16th century. The name 'Fountain' had been passed down through the generations. Amy signed her letter to Rodin using a derivation of this: Amy Mary Fountaine-Elwin. Amy may have met Fountain through his grandfather's connections to Somerset, as Rev Whitwell Elwin was ordained a Deacon at Wells Cathedral in 1839 and then became Curate at Hardington. The 1891 census records the young couple living at Melcombe Regis in Dorset, but ten years later the census gives their address as the Manor House, Booton in Norfolk where generations of the Elwin family had lived. They did not have children and Amy died in 1941 without a will. Fountain died two years later leaving his estate and the residue of his property to Lady Emily Lutyens, the wife of architect Sir Edwin Lutyens, and their son Robert.

I cannot believe that Amy Singer, the clever 'cheery girl' that Thornycroft describes, who spent many happy years in Paris at the epicentre of the art world would have lived so quietly in rural Norfolk and not have made her mark or left an impression there. I shall be continuing research and my focus this year is on Norfolk and searching for Amy's sculptures: in particular the portrait bust of John Webb Singer she is working on in her studio.

[1]*Sue Bucklow, Casting the World: The Story of JW Singer & Sons, of Frome, Rook Lane Arts Trust, 2019*

The Aldefeld* Francisca

An Investigation into the Saxon Origins of Spring Gardens
by Robert Heath

Background

Many of you may have read my article in *Frome Society Yearbook 19*, Exhuming Oldfield[1], in which I described the unusual history of Marston Mill in Spring Gardens. The main conclusions, in reverse order, were as follows:

1 The area known today as Spring Gardens was until the late 19th century called Oldfield, and lay in a detached portion of Marston Bigot. Marston Mill, in use until 1976, was similarly called Oldfield Mill. It was converted to a corn mill in 1820, before which, it had been a tucking mill, used for waterproofing woollen cloth by the fulling process.

2 The mill appears to have been built around 1750 by Joseph Jeffries, to replace an earlier mill. Joseph Jeffries inherited the Oldfield estate from his mother Susannah Jeffries, who inherited it from her father, Francis Joyce, who in turn inherited it from his father, John Joyce. John Joyce's lease was dated around 1630, and was for a fulling mill *and* a dwelling house in Oldfield.

3 Four hundred years earlier, an entry in the Cirencester Cartulary refers to a Richard Bigot, who lived at Aldefeld*(ie Oldfield), bequeathing the proceeds of his mill to Cirencester Abbey, sometime between 1225 and 1233. We concluded from this that the earlier mill was probably not attached to the dwelling house, but was sited at a place known as Five Hatches, around 170 yards north- east of the present mill. Here there had clearly been a structure of some substance, but we had no hard evidence to say it was a mill.

* Note that the previous article erroneously refers to this as Aldfeld

11

4   One curiosity is that there was no mention of either Oldfield or Aldefeld in the Domesday Book. Since we knew that Richard Bigot inherited the main Marston Bigot estate when his brother Robert died childless, we wondered if perhaps the area was referred to as Oldfield because it was the original home of the Bigots before they took over the main Marston estate (ie their 'Old' Field).

Shortly after the publication of Exhuming Oldfield, we were approached by Clive Wilkes, who had a copy of a 1754 lease that described an agreement between *Joseph Jeffrey, Fuller, of Oldfeild (sic) Mill, and Richard Champneys,* to construct a channel to irrigate the Orchardleigh fields further down towards Oldford. The wording on the lease stated the intention ... *to erect flood gates and flood hatches in the mill pond ... and enjoy the free use of water for watering the lands of Richard Champneys at all times whenever the same can be spared from the necessary use of the mills...*   This lease clearly referred to the building of the sluices at Five Hatches, as this is where the still-visible channel running along the valley to the Orchardleigh water meadows starts. What is significant is that it refers to the part of the river at the start of the drainage channel as a *millpond.* If there was a millpond at Five Hatches, there must surely have been a mill!

Aldefeld Mill

With strong evidence that Five Hatches was the likely site of the original Oldfield Mill, the next question was to try to find out when the mill had been built. Clearly it had been there in 1225, but its absence from Domesday suggests it would have been built after 1087. Indeed, what seemed even more strange is that there is no record of Aldefeld at all in Domesday, which suggests the entire estate was established after 1087.

It was then we realised that our theory about the Bigot's calling the area Aldefeld because it was their 'Old Field' made no sense at all, for the following reason:

The word Ald or Alde derives from Old High German dating between 750 and 1050, and attached to a field name describes *land long cultivated or formerly used, ie worn-out or fallow, cf dial old-land arable land left unused* and also *ground that has lain untilled a long time, and is now ploughed up.*[2] The word Feld is also Old High German of the same period, and means ... *open country, unencumbered ground, as distinct from woodland, land used for pasture or cultivation...*[3]   Thus Aldefeld is a <u>Saxon</u> word, which would have been imported into our language when the Saxons invaded England in the 5th century. On reflection it seems highly unlikely that a holding that dated from *after* the Norman Conquest would be given a Saxon-derived name by a Norman nobleman; and even more unlikely that it would be given a name that translates as Old Field, if the holding was only established after the conquest!

So where exactly does this name come from?

The Cirencester Cartulary

The reference to the name Aldefeld is in the Cirencester Cartulary. This is a mediaeval manuscript containing transcriptions of original documents relating to the foundation, privileges, and legal rights of the Abbey. These documents are all in Latin, and published versions tend to summarise the meaning of the text at the start of each entry. For example, the entry 151/83, dated somewhere between 1160-1176, is summarised as *Confirmation by*

Alexander III to the Abbot and Chapter of Cirencester of their church of Marston Bigot, Somerset; and a contemporary entry 605 is summarised as *Charter of Richard son of Odo giving to the canons of Cirencester his church of Marston Bigot, etc.*

From these entries one might assume that the Bigots occupied the Marston estate from as early as 1160, else how would it have become known as Marston Bigot? But when you study the Latin transcript, what is translated as Marston Bigot is actually written just as *Merstun*. In fact, there is no reference to Bigot (or Bigod) in either of the entries 151/83 or 605. The same is true of entry 606, dated 1174-82: the estate is called Marston Bigot in the summary, but written as *Merstuna* in this original Latin. So it looks likely that the Bigots didn't arrive at Marston until towards the end of the 12th century.

The entry 605 does however refer to a gift of the tithes of a Marston parishioner called 'Robert of Buckland' to Cirencester Abbey. Michael McGarvie suggests that Robert of Buckland's holding, which would have been near to Buckland Dinham, was probably our land in Spring Gardens[4], although the name Aldefeld is not mentioned. In fact, the name Aldefeld appears only once, in entry 596, dated between 1225 and 1233. A copy of the entry is shown below in *Fig 1.*

The original Latin text says that Ricardo Bygod (sic) is giving ... *omnibus aliis que emergere possint de quarta parte unius virgate terre et uno molendino cum pertinenciis apud Aldefeld...*, so there is no question that the place being referred to is called Aldefeld. The summary of the entry is also correctly translated as:

> *Quitclaim by Richard Bigot of Oldfield to the abbot and convent of Cirencester of all rights to a fourth part of a virgate and in a mill at Oldfield, except the foreign payment and 4 lb of wax rendered yearly to the chapel at Langley*

But what is most interesting is that the heading of this entry reads *Carta Ricardi Bygod de Aldefeld*, in other words, 'Charter of Richard of Aldefeld': That means that Richard Bigot styled himself as being 'of *Aldefeld*': not Oldfield, but Aldefeld.

As I mentioned earlier, we knew that Richard of Aldefeld inherited the Marston Bigot estate when his brother Robert died childless. One has to observe that it is quite strange for a Norman lordling, heir to a substantial estate the name of which has itself been *changed* to incorporate his family's surname, to use a Saxon name to describe his place of habitation. There can really only be one explanation, which is that the place he lived in was already called Aldefeld. What is more, this place must surely have been in use as a 'Feld' (ie cleared pasture or area of cultivation) for many years, certainly well before the Norman conquest, in order to merit the use of the adjective 'Alde' ie Old.

All of this suggests that, although not referenced in Domesday, there was nevertheless a Saxon estate of some kind in Spring Gardens called Aldefeld.

It was at this point we made a most important discovery.

596

Quitclaim by Richard Bigot of Oldfield to the abbot and convent of Cirencester of all right in a fourth part of a virgate and in a mill at Oldfield, except the foreign payment and 4 lb. of wax rendered yearly to the chapel of Langley. (c. 1225-33)

CARTA RICARDI BYGOD DE ALDEFELD'[1]

Omnibus Christi fidelibus presens scriptum visuris vel audituris Ricardus Bigod salutem in Domino. Noverit universitas vestra me pro salute anime mee et antecessorum meorum et heredum meorum remisisse et quietumclamasse pro me et heredibus meis in perpetuum Deo et ecclesie beate Marie Cyrencestr' et canonicis ibidem Deo servientibus totum jus et clamium quod habui vel aliquo modo habere potui in serviciis debitis, scilicet in homagiis, releviis, wardis, sectis, eschaetis, et omnibus aliis que emergere possint de quarta parte unius virgate terre et uno molendino cum pertinenciis apud Aldefeld' in liberam elemosinam quam Alicia filia Petri Panel[2] tenuit, habendum et possidendum dictis ecclesie et canonicis Cyrencestr' bene et in pace, libere quiete et integre, salvo michi et heredibus meis forinseco ita quod qui pro tempore fuerit custos domus de Langel' forinsecum recipiet de predicta Alicia et heredibus suis et illud persolvet michi et heredibus meis ex parte dictorum canonicorum, et salvis iiij. libris cere capelle de Langel' quas predicta Alicia et heredes sui solvere tenentur annuatim dicte capelle in Nativitate beate Marie. Et ut hec mea remissio et quietaclamacio rata et stabilis inperpetuum permaneat eam hac presenti carta mea confirmavi et sigilli mei impressione roboravi. Hiis testibus W. Broth', Galfrido de Laverton', Roberto de Columbar', Roberto de Meysy, magistro Radulfo de Latton', Thoma de Sodynton', Ricardo rectore ecclesie de Hynglescumbia, Reginaldo vicario de Preston', Ernaldo de From', Hugone Benne et multis aliis.

[1] This document is duplicated in no. 620, where the heading runs : *Carta Ricardi Bigod de Aldefeld juxta Frome de quarta parte unius virgate terre.* [2] *Painel* 620.

MS : A fo. 156v.

Richard Bigot or Bigod held land in Marston Bigot, south of Frome, and was still living in 1243 (*Som. Pleas, Richard I*-41 *Henry III*, pp. 113, 145, 168), but had been succeeded by his son, Hugh, in 1256 (no. 608). Robert of Meisy, who held in Hants. and Wilts. of the honour of Gloucester, was dead by 4 Feb. 1233 (*Exc. e Rot. Fin.*, i, 237 ; *Bk. Fees*, 706-7, 749), and it is probable that this charter is of similar date to no. 599, *q.v.*

Fig 1 The Cirencester Cartulary # 596

The Aldefeld Francisca

A chance encounter with an old acquaintance, Mike McGuinness, in a garden centre in Bath, revealed he had recently taken up metal detecting. I therefore invited him to investigate our land in Spring Gardens. Past metal detecting had supposedly yielded a Georgian silver spoon and a Roman coin, both now missing, but metal detecting equipment has moved on considerably from when the last survey was done some two decades ago.

14

Mike's initial investigation yielded a number of not-very-old coins, some bits of slag, and huge numbers of rather dreary nails and bits of agricultural metalwork. To cut through the noise of the multifarious bits of worthless iron, he switched to just investigating non-ferrous signals, and after several days found an interesting supposedly non-ferrous signal. After digging down some 19 inches, this turned out to be yet another large lump of iron, this time a small but very heavy axe head, and not just any old axe head.

Mike quickly recognised this as a Saxon Throwing Axe, or Francisca, the design of which suggested a date between 450 to 500 AD. This was something of a surprise, as conventional wisdom has it that the Saxons did not reach this far west until around 600 AD. However, Matt Bunker, an expert in this field, confirmed that this design of axe was almost identical to one found in a late Roman shore fort at Burgh Castle, which has been dated to early 5th century. In *Fig 2* below, a sketch is shown of this 5th century Francisca (left) alongside the more traditional 7th century Francisca (right), and the similarity of the design of the earlier example with our Francisca is evident.

Metallurgical analysis has confirmed that it is, in fact, iron, with possibly some steel as well. It was found completely by chance: even modern metal detectors struggle to get a signal from anything buried as deep as 19 inches and had it not erroneously shown up as being non-ferrous, Mike admits he would probably not have bothered to dig it up at all!

This is potentially a find of national significance since only about a dozen Franciscas have been found in the UK. It casts a completely new light on the past history of our location. We now had an important Saxon artefact turning up in an area bearing a Saxon name, which surely suggests Aldefeld must have been a Saxon settlement of some kind. That takes us back to the recurring question: why is there no record of Aldefeld in Domesday, or indeed in any other Saxon charters?

Early 5th Century   *7th Century*

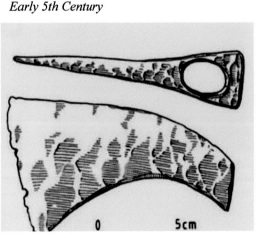 

Fig 2 Francisca Design Burgh Castle

The Domesday Dilemma

There are two possible theories to explain the absence of Aldefeld in Domesday. The first is that the site was out of use in 1087, and therefore merited no entry. That seems unlikely, if the area had enough intrinsic value for Robert of Buckland to rent it just 70 odd years after Domesday. What is more, the very fact that it was called Aldefeld suggests it was a cleared area going back many years, which would hardly to have escaped the notice of William the Conqueror's beady-eyed agents when they examined this area of Somerset for the Domesday record.

The second theory is that Aldefeld was already owned by another Manor, and was therefore included in their return. There is no mention of an Aldefeld in Buckland Dinham or Frome or Orchardleigh, nor in any other adjacent Manor, so the best explanation is that Aldefeld must have already been part of Marston in 1087.

The translated Domesday return for Marston Bigot reads as follows (It needs to be stressed that the name Marston Bigot is yet again a mistranslation, and the estate is referred to simply as Marston):

Marston Bigot: (Land of Roger Arundel) Roger holds Marston (Bigot) himself. Aethelfrith held it before 1066; it paid tax for 3.5 hides. Land for 5 ploughs. In lordship 1 plough; 2 slaves; 1.5 hides. 5 villagers and 14 smallholders have 5 ploughs & 2 hides. A mill which pays 6s; meadow, 16 acres; pasture, 100 acres; woodland one league long and as wide; 9 cattle; 14 pigs; 9 sheep. Value £7; when Roger acquired it £6

So the Manor of Marston mainly comprised woodland (around 9 square miles of it) with 3½ hides of land under cultivation. A hide in Anglo-Saxon times could have been anywhere between 60 and 120 acres, so there would have been some 200 to 400 acres being cultivated. In addition to the forest and cultivated land, Marston had a mill worth 6s, a meadow of 16 acres, and 100 acres pasture. This corresponds roughly to the size of the Aldefeld estate, so if this part of the Domesday entry describes the mill and land at Aldefeld, it would explain why Aldefeld is not in Domesday. The mill worth 6s, could also explain why this detached portion of land, about 3 miles away from the main estate was deemed worthy of being retained at all.

Mill Valuations

Some useful information can be derived from looking at the value of the Domesday Marston mill compared with its neighbours. The way that the Domesday commissioners valued mills was generally in line with the water flow of the stream they stood on, and it has always been assumed that the mill at Marston was on the River Frome, at Iron Mill near Witham Hall.[5] However, the river flow in this section of the Frome is really very modest: the river is barely more than 2½ miles from its source at Cannwood, and there are no evident signs of other mill sites in mediaeval Marston that could have justified a value of 6s in Domesday. There *is* a disused mill site at Bull's Bridge, Tytherington, and another further downstream at Blatchbridge, but both of these lie outside the mediaeval Marston holding.

Robert Arkell, who has studied closely the Domesday references to mills in the Frome area, is inclined to the view that Oldfield is a more likely site for the Marston Domesday mill.

He notes that Reinbald's mill further downstream on the Frome from the Marston main estate, is valued only at 5s, and the higher value mills in Frome itself, which benefit from the additional flow of the Rodden, are only 7s 6d and 8s 4d. In contrast, he observes that the Marston value of 6s is consistent with mills upstream on the Mells (Great Elm 4s 2d, Mells 5s, Holcombe 6d). Also, the Oldfield site benefits from the flow of the Nunney brook, which had a mill valued at 2s 6d, and the Whatley brook, which had a 5s mill. Finally, the mill at Oldford, downstream from Oldfield, which has the combined flow of the Frome and Mells rivers, was valued at 7s 6d. In other words, a value of 6s is almost exactly what you would expect from a mill located at Aldefeld.

So using mill values there is a fairly good case for Aldefeld being the mill in the Marston Domesday return and even if it is not, and the mill was indeed built post Domesday, it does seem likely that Aldefeld was owned by Marston, which is why it does not appear in Domesday.

So what if anything do we know about Saxon Aldefeld?

Saxon Aldefeld

BACAS (Bath and Counties Archaeological Society) commenced an investigation in autumn 2019 into the area around where the Francisca was discovered. Initial geophysics results suggest an area of occupation with numerous embankments and post-holes, and signs of buildings. They have also found some Saxon pottery dated between 600 and 800 AD, some Roman pottery and a large number of Mesolithic flints. This suggests the occupation of Aldefeld might go back much further than even Saxon times.

Why might Aldefeld be chosen as a place to live? A number of factors make it attractive.

Firstly, the topography of Aldefeld is especially good for a settlement. A topographical map of the area using Lidar data (*Fig 3*) shows a distinct area, shaded blue, of what would once have been water meadow, at the junction of the Mells Brook and the River Frome. Besides this, is a larger slightly higher area, which would make a perfect encampment.

Secondly, Aldefeld is located on the boundary between Wessex, the west Saxon county, and Hwicce, which was the final defensive outpost of post-Roman British occupation. Cerdic is recorded as becoming the first king of Wessex in 519, but the Anglo-Saxon Chronicle claims that he landed in Hampshire as early as 495. These dates accord with the date of our Francisca.

Thirdly, the topography of Aldefeld is attractive as a defensive position, lying as it does in a natural dip between Selwood Forest to the South and the Mendips to the North. Anyone one wishing to carry goods from Wells eastward would find the valley of the Mells an attractive and relatively low-lying route, and Aldefeld a convenient stop-off in which to graze their livestock, and, for the Saxons who arrived late in the 5th century, it might be an extremely good place to ambush passing traffic!

Studying *Fig 3* shows that Oldfield Hall House in fact lies on exactly the same contour as Aldefeld Mill, above the flood plain. The mill siting is especially appropriate, as the Mells Brook runs along the side of the northern escarpment, and at the point where the mill turns south into the flood plain: in effect, a natural site for a mill.

17

Incidentally, Richard of Aldefeld's gift to Cirencester included a 'fourth part' of a virgate. A virgate is generally reckoned as being 30 acres, so his bequest would have been about 7 – 8 acres. That is almost exactly the area of the water meadows shown in *Fig 3*. So perhaps it was these that he generously donated to Cirencester, along with the proceeds of Aldefeld Mill, when he succeeded to the much greater estate of Marston Bigot?

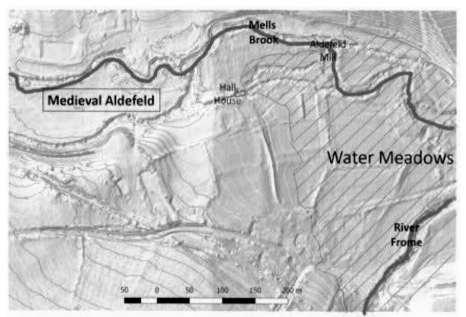

Fig 3 Topography of Aldefeld

The 400 year gap

Using the 1839 Tithe Map of the Parish of Marston Bigot in conjunction with the 1925 Ordnance Survey, is appears that the total Oldfield estate covered some 168 acres. Twenty seven of these were to the west of the A361 and south of the road to Mells, adjacent to Vallis Farm; 21 were in the area now occupied by Somerleaze, south of the site of Murtry Mill; 76 acres were north of the Mells Brook in the area of Brookover Farm; and just 44 were in what is now Spring Gardens. So what happened to this extensive estate between Richard Bigot leaving around 1230, and John Joyce's lease of 1630?

The Tax Rolls of Edward III, compiled in Latin in 1327, mention a Hugone le Bole working at Marston Bigot with 14 men below him, and a Jacobo de Molyn also working in Marston Bigot with 6 men listed below him. Since Jacobo de Molyn means James Miller in English, it seems probable that he and his 6 companions were working at Oldfield,[6] but thereafter there are no records at all. We know that towards the end of the 14th century the Bigots had gone, and the Marston Estate was taken into ownership by the Stourtons, and presumably they must have been responsible for the extension to Oldfield Hall in 1507. Why they did this is not clear, but since the old manor on the Marston Estate was at the time ..*a glorified farmhouse (as) it had been in the middle ages... plainly called Marston*

18

Farm, or the Farm House,[7] it may be that the Stourtons extended Oldfield Hall to use as their own occasional residence. Unfortunately the Stourtons proved a disreputable bunch, and when William Stourton was hanged in 1557 for murdering William Hartgill, his estate was forfeited to the crown.[8] It was let out to various occupants, then in 1596 sold to William Brown and James Orenge. By 1600 Orenge owned it outright, and being a speculator, he compiled a detailed survey to assist in its sale. Although the original of this valuation has been lost, a copy was made of it in 1745 by the Earl of Cork, and Michael McGarvie has very kindly entrusted us with the last remaining photocopy of this copy.

What is immediately evident from Orenge's valuation is that by 1600 Oldfield had shrunk to around 75 acres. In an area known as Mortrofer (in 1745 referred to as Broksover, and now Brookover) around 60 acres had been let to Richard Champneys of Orchardleigh for a peppercorn rent and a further 30 acres north of the Mells were let to him at a heavily discounted rate of just 1 shilling 6 pence per acre. Interestingly there is no mention of any mill in the Marston Estate.

We know that the marriage settlement in 1605 between John Champneys and Honor Chaldecott cites him owning *...two fullinge mills in Oldfielde within the pishe (parish) of Marston Bigott alias Marston Bigood* [9]... so evidently Oldfield Mill was sold to Champneys before the Orenge valuation. This transfer of the mill to Champneys is confirmed by a mention in the Orenge valuation of some 7 acres of land adjacent to 'John Taylor's Mill', north of the Mells, being <u>excluded</u> from Oldfield. We were rather confused by this, until we noticed that John Taylor is in fact shown in the Orchardleigh records as an alias for John Joyce, who had his lease on a mill and dwelling renewed by the Champneys around 1630.[10]

So where is Oldfield Hall in the Orenge valuation? In the entries for Oldfield there is one which is described as follows:

> *One great feeding close called Barnclose wherein a house Standith bounded with the lane towards Hills mill on the north and west side and water (Mells Brook) on the north wherein is said to be about 3 acres of (blank) land containing 30 acres at 10s =13.1.*

Hills Mill seems to be Murtry Mill, and the 'water' referred to is the Mells Brook, so this Barnclose is effectively where Spring Gardens is now, and since this is the only mention of a house in the whole Oldfield valuation it seems very likely it is Oldfield Hall. However, nothing is said of the occupancy of this house, nor do any of the tenancies mentioned in the valuation refer to it. Since the Earl of Cork's 1745 notes say that the 3 acres are excluded from any rent, it looks likely that this house might also have already been sold to the Champneys, and given its proximity to John Taylor / Joyce's mill it would almost certainly have been the dwelling house referred to in his 1630 lease.

Summary

The 'prequel' to Exhuming Oldfield now looks like this:

1   The presence of Mesolithic flints and Roman pottery suggests Spring Gardens has been occupied on and off for thousands of years.

2   It seems likely that sometime in the 5th or 6th century a party of Saxon invaders arrived at this area. Recognising the value of the water meadows and the proximity to the border of the Hwicce, an area still held by the Romano British, they decided to settle here.

3   They may perhaps have had a skirmish there with their enemies, during which one of them lost his throwing axe, or the trusty weapon may have been buried with one of their number. Either way, at some stage the area was cleared and occupied, and after many years the by-now-ancient settlement became known as Aldefeld.

4   At some point-in-time a mill was built. Perhaps because of this mill, or perhaps just because of its value as a holding, Aldefeld was incorporated into the much larger Manor at Merstun (Marston), a few miles away. This may have been during Aethelfrith's ownership, or even earlier.

5   Following the conquest of Britain by William, Aethelfrith's estate was given to Roger of Arundel, who was the Lord of the Manor when the Domesday accounting took place in 1087.

6   In 1160, Roger Arundel rented Aldefeld to Robert of Buckland, giving the tithes from this rental to Cirencester Abbey.

7   A few years later, certainly before 1195, the Manor of Marston passed to Richard Bigot (1), and was renamed Marston Bigot.

8   Richard died and passed his estate to his eldest son Robert,who allowed his younger brother Richard (2) to take over the detached portion of the Marston Bigot estate at Aldefeld. Richard must have been quite proud of his small estate, because he styled himself 'Richard of Aldefeld'. Possibly there was a timber dwelling house there, dating from Robert of Buckland's time, which Richard demolished and replaced with a stone hall house, appointing Peter Panel to operate his mill.

9   On the death of his childless brother, Richard succeeded to the Marston Bigot estate sometime between 1225 and 1233. To increase his chances of getting to paradise, he bequeathed the proceeds of Aldefeld Mill, which by now was operated by Peter's daughter, Alice Panel, and the adjacent water meadows, to Cirencester Abbey.

10 In 1507 Richard's hall house was extended by the Stourtons into a proper country house with the addition to the Hall of a kitchen and storeroom , with a substantial great chamber above.

11 Sometime before 1600 Oldfield Mill and Hall were transferred to Orchardleigh together with large areas of farmland to the north of Mells Brook. By 1600 the mill was operated by John Joyce, alias Taylor, and in 1630 he renewed his lease for both the mill and Oldfield Hall. Thereafter the history can be traced in my previous article 'Exhuming Oldfield'[1]

Finally, in order to try to establish when Oldfield Hall House was first built, some samples of wood from the redundant roof truss in the mediaeval hall section have been sent for radiocarbon dating. Sadly, due to the Covid 19 pandemic, the laboratory processing these was closed a week before the results were due, so we shall have to report these findings in a future edition of the Yearbook.

[1] *Robert Heath, Exhuming Oldfield, FSLS Yearbook 19, 2016*
[2] https://en.wiktionary.org/wiki/alde
[3] https://en.wiktionary.org/wiki/Feld
[4] *Michael McGarvie, The Book of Marston Bigot, Barracuda Books, 1987, p27*
[5] *ibid p17*
[6] *ibid p29*
[7] *ibid p35*
[8] *ibid p32*
[9] *DD\SOG/752*
[10] *DD\DU/33*

Silk Factory

The chimney of the new silk mill has been completed and is now, from its style, as well as from its intended use, an interesting feature in the aspect of the Town from many points of view. Its form is octagonal rising to a height of 130 feet and is surmounted by an elegant Italian cupola and reflects great credit to Mr Joseph Chapman who was both architect and builder. We understand the octagonal shaft was laid during the Whitsun week and has been erected throughout the week without the aid of stimulants on the part of the workmen in the way of strong drink.

Somerset and Wilts Journal, 28 June 1856

Frome

Strike of Carpenters and Joiners: The arbitration between the builders of this town and the carpenters and joiners in their employ has fallen to the ground, and on Saturday last the union and non-union men alike struck work for an advance of 2s per week in the rate of wages and a reduction of hours to 54 per week. The masters are willing to concede the former, but they firmly refuse to yield the nine hours' movement. These are the terms which compromise with the masons was arranged. The men feel sore at the delay (three weeks) that has taken place since the masters and themselves agreed to refer the dispute to the arbitration of Mr Barnden, of Warminster. It is hoped by the time of the Whitsun holidays are over the affair will be amicably and satisfactorily arranged.

My thanks to ALM for this extract from the Southern Times 30 May 1874. Ed

Catholic Education from 1850-1950 at the Conigar, Frome

by Shelagh Fearnehough

Today, Apex House has been developed into seven private apartments, but local records point to a history when it was known as Conigar House, and almost entirely occupied by religious women caring for the poor and educating children.

Apex House as modern apartments in 2019.The Home School structure on the left is still clear today.

It started with Rev William James Early Bennett, the controversial Anglican priest, and some dedicated women followers from his London parish. They made this house their base for parish work and a Home School until 1878. Later, in 1902, the French Roman Catholic

Sisters of Charity of St Louis arrived, establishing St Louis Convent School and orphanage here until it was sold in 1968 to JW Singer & Sons.

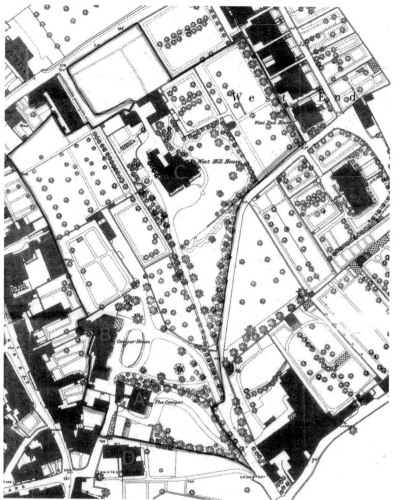

The town Map of 1886 shows the Conigar area and the position of The Conigar(A), Conigar House(B), West Hill House(C), and the Roman Catholic Church(D) together with probable garden land

The Conigar area of Frome is south of Cork Street, on a hillside below Milk Street. The definition of 'conigar' is rabbit warren and the early mediaeval English term is conygarth.

This area originally formed part of land of the Manor of St Katherine and remained relatively intact until the 18th century, used as pasture land for grazing sheep and the cultivation of woad for dyeing cloth.[1]

In the early 1800s the Conigar became fashionable, and this is where Edward Barnard built his gracious house known as The Conigar. The house was built before 1810, then acquired during the 1830s by the Attorney of the County Court, George Messiter and his family. It seems likely that Messiter built Conigar House in the late 1840s, on the substantial land to the west of his family home[2]. It stood in an elevated position, with nearly an acre of grounds, outbuildings and approached by a carriage drive. The census in 1851 records it as 'uninhabited', but it was occupied soon after, and extended to accommodate Bennett's St John the Baptist Home School for orphans and poor children.

Bennett arrived in Frome in December 1851, having accepted the appointment to the living at St John's Parish Church. His controversial years in the fashionable parish of St Paul's, Knightsbridge with its extremes of poverty and wealth had ended. The High Church ancient rituals caused a stir and the nature of his sermons and rioting in his parish, eventually led to Bennett's resignation.

Rev WJE Bennett (1804-1886)

Anglican Parish Sisterhood

During 1849 there were many accusations made against Bennett by the Bishop of London, including reference to a religious community of laywomen, the Sisterhood, which Bennett was attempting to establish in St Paul's parish. Before long there was dreadful gossip from parishioners that he was taking women away from their home duties: and receiving 'sisters' from wealthy families against the wishes of their parents[3].

At least three women of status came to Frome to work with Bennett. They were Alexandrine Perceval Ouseley (1814-1862), her sister Mary Jane (1806- 1861) and Agnes Logan Stewart (1820-1886). Bennett's connection with them and their distinguished, rich families began when they worshipped at St Paul's, and generously contributed to the building of St Barnabas Church and schoolhouse for the poor in Pimlico.

In the 19th century wealthy women were expected to marry, have children and live an easy life. Unlike today, to remain single was thought a disgrace, therefore parents were anxious to see their daughters marry. Alexandrine and Mary never married, despite being expected to play their part in society, including the London Season where they would attend balls and soirées for the purpose of attracting worthy suitors[4], however Agnes was fully prepared to enter society: she was charming, tutored in music and dancing was one of her main interests. At twenty-three years old, she gave all this up in readiness for a life of devotion to those in need.

These women had a strong wish for the religious life and had approached Bennett for his help. They worked tirelessly in the parish Sisterhood, visiting those families living in extreme deprivation in the slums of Pimlico. They gained skills and experience in nursing, teaching and an understanding of poverty and social welfare. The creation of the Anglican Sisterhood at that time, gave holy employment for many single women who could channel their female religious zeal[5].

The accusations against Bennett were eventually dropped, but he accepted that the St Paul's Sisterhood had been premature, however something of the kind was established at Conigar House. This began in 1852 when Alexandrine and Mary Ouseley arrived in Frome. They settled at Conigar House, followed a spiritual life and they lived together with every characteristic as a Sisterhood in all but the name.

In a biographical note in the *Somerset Standard,* JW Singer wrote that the sisters, through their own choice, wore simple clothes during their residence here: *...they looked and dressed like they belonged to a Sisterhood*[6] *without any connection with one...*

The sisters came to Frome to help Bennett. They had the determination and commitment to improve the lives of the poor and sick. The result was the remarkable organization of parish services including home visits, soup kitchens, access to medical help and a charity shop selling clothing at a small sum to the poor.

According to Singer, Alexandrine was the most gifted of the sisters, described as: *...one of the most saintly women for truly working entirely for others.* She devoted herself totally to works of charity with no thought of reward or public appreciation.

Later a religious Sisterhood gained church approval and was established in Frome. In 1857 Agnes Logan Stewart joined Bennett here; after a time of entirely devoting herself, and her inheritance, to God's service, both at St Paul's and St John's, Agnes sought consent from him and became a religious Sister.

She founded a small religious community of women, and in 1871 Mother Agnes was leading a Sisterhood at Conigar House with Sarah Jane Mason, Mary Giles and Betsy Smith. The four women are described as 'Sisters of Mercy' in the census record and lived together with nine girl boarders, aged between eight and thirteen, with two governesses, six servants and three teachers.

Home School

The Home School was under Bennett's management. It was first established in the late 1850s at 26 Chappell Street (Whittox Lane) under the care of Alexandrine and Mary. Alexandrine used her fortune to extend Conigar House to make it into the Home for twelve orphan girls, and had a schoolroom built for the children of the poor to be educated.

This was at a time when there was much poverty, high numbers of orphaned, unwanted children and children whose parents could not afford to keep them living in the family. By the 1861 census the Home School operated from both Chappell Street and Conigar House, with thirteen girl boarders and house servants. The Sisters are both described as the 'School Holders'.

Sister of Mercy, Agnes Logan Stewart

These young girls living at the Home had their spiritual and physical needs met by Alexandrine and Mary. They would be well cared for, fed and clothed.

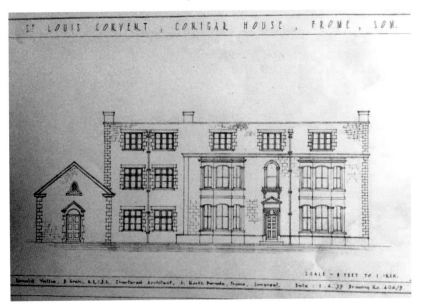

Frome Architect Ronald Vallis' 1939 plans for St Louis Convent of Conigar House clearly show the original c1849 structure, and the Home School extension that includes the schoolroom, 1862

The school was called 'Free School' as no charge was made. This was one of the first free schools in the country and maintained by voluntary contributions, mainly from Alexandrine's inheritance. The education of the children of the lowest class was dedicated to teaching practical skills that would help them earn money honestly and improve lives: training for domestic service, sewing, laundry and cleaning and preparation for working in the factories. Children were taught rigorously about religion, to read and study the bible and be virtuous.

In July 1861 Mary died aged 54. Alexandrine carried on with the same quiet endeavour, running the Home School and her charity work with the poor until it overwhelmed her. In December 1862 she died of a fever. Children from the Home School attended her funeral and six young girls were pallbearers[7]. Following her death, Mother Agnes and her Sisters of Mercy, took charge of the Home School and moved to Conigar House. Agnes was described as having a natural talent for helping others[8]. Not only did women and men of the parish go to her with their troubles, but she set up mothers' meetings and bible classes.

It seems that her responsibilities increased, because in 1866, Samuel Cuzner lists a Free School attached to St Mary's Church, and the Girls Free School and Home at Conigar House, all presided over by 'Mother Superior and Sisters of the Home'[9].

By late 1871 Mother Agnes had left for Leeds. She had responded to an advertisement placed in the Church Times calling for women of private means to work in the parish of St Saviour's in Leeds, with a view to a Sisterhood. On her arrival there she purchased and restored three large houses to create an orphanage. Once the work was completed, she brought some of her Sisters and orphans from the Home in Frome to join her.

After her departure the Home School continued under Sister Mary Giles and Sister Marie Albin Bailey. It was now known as St John the Baptist's Home which as well as a Free School and Home, now offered a day nursery for infants so their mothers could work.

Sister Mary died in 1877 and a year later the Home School closed. Conigar House was put up for sale, however it seems it was not sold, as George Messiter's son Frederick, conveyed the house and land to John Webb Singer in 1880. For a short time between 1881-1889, the house was a family home: widower William Tonkin, a Silk Merchant, and his young family were tenants. By 1891 Augusta Ellen Bennett lived here until she died in 1902. She was the late Rev Bennett's daughter and a parish worker. In parallel, The Conigar was occupied by Herbert Singer and his family during the 1880s.

Roman Catholic Sisters of the Charity of St Louis

In 1902 a French order, the Sisters of St Louis first arrived in Frome. Mother Therese, Mother Fidele and the Sisterhood made their home and private school at Melrose House. This was soon found to be too small and, following the death of Augusta Bennett, they chose Conigar House. The house was close to the Roman Catholic Church and presbytery, and when they moved into their new Convent and school in 1903, they were already part of the community.

The order had been founded in Brittany in 1803 to take care of orphaned and deserted children. In1900 French anticlericalism drove out French Catholic orders and many fled to England. This order had already opened a successful Convent and school in Minehead. Their priorities were the education of Roman Catholic children and they offered a strict religious system of morals. The Sisters had already brought some orphans and boarders with them from France. They were soon advertising a 'high- class school' for girls as boarders, and both boys and girls as day scholars.

This was not a 'free school' and many families who sent their children were not well off. Cash flow and financial resources were often a problem; the Sisters relied on the Roman Catholic Diocese of Clifton, benefactors and fee-paying scholars to enable their Convent school to grow[10].

Conigar House, The Schoolhouse c1920

Unlike the previous Anglican Sisterhood who had their own wealth, these Sisters needed to support themselves, earn a living by their own efforts to fund their religious life and their charitable work. They undertook needlework and embroidery. Private lessons of French, music and painting were offered and attracted scholars who had the means to pay for education. Lay Sisters offered sewing to the poorer children and laundry work.

Despite the financial difficulties, St Louis Convent School and orphanage began to grow steadily and successfully. In 1905 the Sisters purchased Conigar House on a mortgage, and two properties east and west, as a 'package' from JW Singer and Sons: The Conigar and West Hill House.

The Conigar, The Orphanage c1910

Three grand houses meant the provision of care and education for more children, and a dedicated Convent for the Sisterhood. The 1911 census shows St Louis Convent operating from all three properties with seventy residents.

> Conigar House is described as the schoolhouse, and laundry, with ten female residents.
> The Conigar is described as the orphanage with thirty-nine female residents.
> West Hill House is described as the Convent with twenty female residents and one male (gardener)

Information from the census records the Head as Mother Eudoxie Simon, born in France. All orphans and boarders were Roman Catholic from different areas of the country. Only Gabrielle Turner was born in Frome, and she was the youngest, aged three.

The outbreak of the First War exerted a severe strain on the community. The Mother Superior worked with the Belgian Relief Committee and offered hospitality to Belgian refugees. In 1916 four girls were admitted and taught by the Sisters skills necessary to earn their own livelihood on their return to Belgium.[11]

After the war, the Sisters widened the scope of the school curriculum, including 'special subjects' such as typewriting and shorthand. Funds were made available for a significant extension to West Hill House, adding a Convent chapel, improved dormitories and classrooms.

West Hill House, The Convent with the extension to the left of the original house c2006

During the Second World War all available space was in use: the Sisters, and many families in Frome cared for evacuees from London. In 1939 architect plans by Ronald Vallis, show a vision to enlarge Conigar House by adding a new school hall to seat two hundred and fifty, and improvements to the laundry at West Hill House.

The new hall was never built but there was a new laundry with modern facilities. A busy laundry service was now offered across town and to the American Army Camp based at the Longleat Estate. This significantly increased the income for the Convent, but it was hard work for the young girls working in the laundry during the war years and they recalled long hours and harsh conditions.

Conigar House. St Louis Convent School Photograph c1940

After the war there were changes for St Louis Convent with a reduction in operations. By 1948 the orphanage had closed due to changes in the law for children and families: The Conigar was not required and sold as a private house; It was renamed Conigre House.

The Conigar as Conigre House in 2019

The Sisters continued to use Conigar House for living accommodation until the mid-1960s; it was then bought by Singers and used as office accommodation and renamed Apex House.

The laundry closed during the 1950s and West Hill House became the main school building, with dormitories for boarders at the top of the original house.

This house was used throughout the transition to the new St Louis Voluntary Aided Primary School that was built within the grounds of Conigar House. The school opened in 1970 for day pupils. Sister Mary McMahon was the Acting Head and there were seventy-five children on the school roll. West Hill House was eventually sold and later developed as apartments. It has retained its name.

Conigar House as Apex House as JW Singer offices c1970.

For over a hundred years Conigar House had accommodated communities of religious women carrying out pioneering charitable work and helping families in Frome. Such communities, Anglican and Roman Catholic undertook what was considered then as acceptable women's work: care of the poor and sick, and the education of children, especially girls.

From a modern perspective these women can be seen as firmly rooted in the feminist tradition: committed to supporting women, creating effective organizations, dedicated to education and improving the lives of the poor. These women made an important contribution to the social history of Frome. How fortunate that they chose to make Frome their home!

Acknowledgements

With special thanks to:

Sister Josephine Goggin for sharing her knowledge and memories of St Louis Convent School.
Jane Maryon, Apex House and Elizabeth Roberts, West Hill House for their contribution to the knowledge of the Conigar area.
Frome Museum for the use of their records and library.

References

[1] *Carolyn Griffiths, Woad to This, FSLS, 2017*
[2] *Michael McGarvie,The Biography of Arthur Messiter. FSLS Yearbook 13, 2009*
[3] *F Bennett, The Story of WJE Bennett. Longmans, Green & Co, 1909*
[4] *J Austine, Ouseley's Legacy, Coxwalker Creative, 2014*
[5] *R Morgan, Sisterhood is Global, Anchor Press, 1984*
[6] *John Webb Singer, Frome Worthies: Alexandrine Percival Ouseley, Somerset Standard, 9 September 1893*
[7] *ALM, From the Czar's Palace, St Petersburg to a Charity Shop in Whittox Lane, Frome, FSLS Yearbook 22, 2019*
[8] *Leeds Civic Trust, A Blue Plaque for 'Mother' Agnes, Diocese of Leeds, 2018*
[9] *S Cuzner, Handbook to Froome Selwood,1866*
[10] *JA Harding, The History of the Roman Catholic Church in Frome 1850-1927, University of Bristol, 1985*
[11] *Gillian Hogarth, The Anglo-Catholic Parsons and the 'Eitalian' Mission, FSLS Yearbook 20, 2017*

Rev George Angus' Visit to Frome

In the year 1868 I spent two or three days at Frome, where is a beautiful church beautifully restored by the then Vicar, Mr Bennett. I and a friend called upon him, and found him cutting out altar breads for next day, it being the titular feast, St John the Baptist. The day before we paid a flying vist to Downside, where we were hospitably entertained...We passed *en route* Whatley, where Dean Church, a great friend of Newman, was Vicar, before he went to St. Paul's. We returned to Frome for Solemn Evensong, sung at the unearthly hour of 9pm. There was a very long procession with the Vicar at its end attired in a cope and holding a hymn book. Next morning, after a bad night caused by the presence of industrious specimens of the *pulex irritants,* or domestic flea, I went to the 9 o'clock High Celebration. Mr Bennett allowed no celebrations after that hour, which he and some other Anglicans thought primitive..... The service at Frome was beautifully rendered, and was followed at 11 o'clock by High Morning Prayer and Sermon, which somehow was dreary..... We then returned to Cheltenham by way of Bath, as I did not want for obvious reasons to try to sleep again in Frome...

My thanks to ALM for this extract from The Tablet, 23 January 1904. Ed

Postcards from the past
by Catherine Hanley

Winifred Tucker in the early 1900s

On Christmas Day 1903, my eighteen-year-old great-grandmother Winifred Tucker (later Winifred Weaver) was given a postcard album. She began to collect cards to put in it almost immediately; the first two are postmarked 31 December 1903, and a number of those dating from 1904 include questions on how much of the album she has filled. Winifred continued to be an avid collector for many years. The bulk of the collection (insofar as it can be dated – some of the cards are blank and thus have no postmark) consists of cards sent between 1904 and 1920, although she continued to add to it sporadically for many years afterwards, by which time the album was full and she stored the cards in a box.

Winifred's postcard album pictured over a century later

Postcards were sent with a much greater frequency in the early 1900s than they are now, being quick and cheap to deliver in an era before use of the telephone was widespread.[1] Many of the cards in the album are in effect the text messages of their day, containing notes such as 'arrived safely, will write tomorrow' or 'arriving Frome station at half past five'. Others are from trips away, perhaps to the seaside or to visit relatives.

The pictures on the front of postcards differed considerably at that time from what we might expect now. Some themes are familiar – attractive views or pictures of notable buildings – but many are photographs of individuals. Photography in the early 20th century was something of a specialised hobby, with those fortunate enough to own a camera having to carry out their own developing;[2] this meant that it was more common for people to have a photograph professionally taken and then made into a postcard to be sent to friends and family. Scenes of local life were also captured for posterity, and the collection contains many depictions of Frome social groups, sports teams, amateur dramatic productions, and so on.

The album is thus not only a family treasure, giving me a personal insight into the everyday thoughts and deeds of my ancestors, but also a wonderful snapshot of life in Frome in the early part of the 20th century. Here, for example, is a marvellous group picture featuring people of all ages:

Sunday school picnic

The word 'picnic' is just visible on the front, and the message on the back helpfully adds that the occasion was a Sunday school outing. Alas, the sender then adds 'Can you see me in the picture?', but without signing his or her name: one of the many frustrations of the modern family history researcher. Another early card is this (happily clearly labelled) image of the Frome YMCA football team in the 1905–6 season:

Frome YMCA football team, 1905–6

The addressee is Winifred's eldest brother, Sidney Herbert (Bert) Tucker, and two of her other brothers would have been the right age to be featured here, but alas, if they are then I am unable to identify them. Here is another sports team from around a quarter of a century later:

Frome rugby club, 1930s

Winifred's eldest son, Graham Weaver (1911–70),[3] is the figure in the back row wearing the white shirt; guessing at his probable age dates this photo to the 1930s, probably the first half of the decade. Does anyone recognise any of the other players or officials?

Amateur dramatics is a theme that occurs frequently in cards that date from after Winifred's marriage to Herbert Edwin (Bert) Weaver in 1909; her husband's family appear to have been keen actors. Two images from Mells, however, serve an additional purpose in highlighting a social change:

'Much Ado About Nothing' (Mells, 1913)   *'The Vicar of Wakefield' (Mells, 1918)*

The figure playing Leonato (with the implausible beard) in the 1913 image is Winifred's brother-in-law Charles (Charlie) Weaver, then a junior schoolmaster in Mells and later the head teacher of Dulverton school for many years. Several other postcards featuring the same play – not pictured here – depict other young men of a similar age, but this is a demographic significantly absent in the 1918 production.

There are, unsurprisingly, many postcards of the First World War era in Winifred's collection; with five brothers, a husband and two brothers-in-law, it must have been a worrying time for her. The imagery featured on postcards during the war is distinctive and falls into three principal types. First is photographs of soldiers, either in regimental groups or standing proudly in studios in their brand new uniforms – some of them disturbingly young-looking. These were evidently meant as mementoes to leave behind them with loved ones; second is the frequent use of cartoons and 'jokes' of a racist, anti-German, 'fighting the Hun' type, and thirdly is what would now be seen as a worrying tendency to militarise society and particularly young children. Pictures of tiny tots in uniforms and/or with guns were commonplace, as is this example:

ARE WE DOWNHEARTED?
NO!

Postcard of 1916 depicting a young boy in military uniform

This card was sent to Winifred's son Graham, then aged 5, by 'Uncle Bruce', Winifred's youngest brother, and the message tells him that 'You must be like the little boy in the picture when the sums don't come right'. Bruce (Robert Bruce Tucker) was at this point a 22-year-old warehouseman; a civilian who, like many others, had joined up to do his bit. He would be killed in action in Flanders in 1918, and I admit that I became quite emotional when I first read of this. It happened over a century ago, but I had spent many weekend afternoons reading through his cheery notes to his siblings and nephew, so I almost felt that I knew him personally. He left a widow and three very young children.

Frome, of course, suffered many losses in the First World War, and a memorial was erected to remember them:

The unveiling of Frome war memorial, 1917

I was surprised to see the date of this ceremony: I am by no means an expert, but had vaguely assumed that most memorials were constructed after the war, in 1919 or 1920. However, the card here clearly shows 1917, and I find from further research that a 'War Shrines Movement' began as early as mid-1916.[4] After the war, Frome slowly returned to normal, its schools, churches and societies thriving:

Staff and pupils of St Louis' RC school, 1920s

Clergy and lay servers of St John's church, 1930s

Frome Ancient Order of Foresters, late 1920s/early 1930s.
All three postcards above include members of Winifred's family.

There are many, many more fascinating images in Winifred's postcard collection, but I will end with a happy family snap that has a definite FSLS connection, even though it was not taken in Frome:

Winifred and family on the promenade at Weymouth, c 1930

Seaside pictures appear frequently on postcards of the 1920s and 1930s; enterprising photographers would snap happy holidaymakers – always smartly dressed, with blazers, ties and hats much in evidence – and then make the resulting images into postcards for them to share with their families and *friends* or to keep as souvenirs. Here Winifred (in the hat) walks with her only sister Beatrice. The boy and smaller girl are Winifred's two youngest children, Raymond (1917–33) and Barbara (1922–2002); the older girl is their cousin and Beatrice's daughter, Eunice Overend (1919–2016), a founder member of FSLS.[3]

[1] *Eric J Evans and Jeffrey Richards, A Social History of Britain in Postcards, 1870-1930, Longman, 1980*
[2] *ALM, Early Camera Clubs in Frome, FSLS Yearbook 21, 2018*
[3] *Catherine Hanley, The Weaver Family of Hemington and Frome, FSLS Yearbook 15, 2012*
[4] *Alex King, Memorials of the Great War in Britain, Berg, 1998*

Dr Catherine Hanley is a historian and the author of several books; she has been researching the history of her Frome and Hemington ancestors for some time, and has been fortunate enough to inherit a huge amount of primary material that she still hasn't worked her way through. Ed

Richard John Munro Dupont
1920-1977
by Janet Howard

The equestrian portrait painter, Richard John Munro Dupont was born in Frome on 20 July 1920, the eldest son of Dr John Munro Dupont (1868-1938) and his wife, Edith Eileen née Kemp (1884-1974). The family lived at Bridge House, Bridge Street, Frome. Dr Dupont was a General Practitioner for nearly 40 years and held his surgery at Bridge House. He and his wife are buried in the churchyard of St John's Church, Frome.

Bridge House, Bridge Street in 2020
Photo: Cliff Howard

Richard Dupont at
Marlborough College 1937
Photo: Marlborough College

Richard Dupont attended Marlborough College from May 1934 to December 1937. The Marlborough College Register records that '*RJM Dupont was placed in the Lower 4th Form when he came to Marlborough in May 1934. He made slow-ish progress through the Lower, Middle and Upper 4th forms and reached the Shell Form (*the lowest form of the Middle School) *in January 1937. He was moved up to the Remove Form in September 1937'* It is fair to say that his strengths at Marlborough were not academic. His artistic talent was however recognised and he was awarded the Lower School Drawing Prize in September 1935 and the Holiday Sketching Prize in the Michaelmas Term of 1937 [1].

In December 1938 Richard Dupont entered the Royal Academy Schools. His studies were interrupted by the Second World War. In 1941 he was commissioned in The Dorsetshire Regiment and was promoted to Lieutenant on 1 October 1942. He mobilised for India in April 1942. The Battalion served with distinction at Kohima and in the Burma campaign. In the book 'March On' by Norman Havers, it is recorded that '*No account of troopship life can be complete without mention of the lectures inflicted on captive audiences, talks that were often more valued for filling gaps in a daily programme than their ability to instruct or entertain. Officers were detailed to hold forth willy-nilly and our battalion would have been about average in having two who were able to do this tiresome job with brilliance, Captain Pryke Howard and Lieutenant Richard Dupont, who performed so well and entertainingly that they are still remembered............Richard, a pupil and disciple of the artist Alfred Munnings was a natural performer and could bring the house down when recounting a generously embroidered account of his life as an art student. Later in the year, when on duty at Ahmadnagar (sic) Fort, using charcoal and colour he decorated the walls of the Officers' Mess with sketches of thoroughbred horses with a skill that brought to life their spirit and beauty.'* [2]

In 1943, Dupont, now a Captain, was appointed an official war artist for the South-East Asia theatre. Three of his paintings of the 1944 Arakan Campaign are in the collection of the Imperial War Museum in London.[3] The charcoal sketch shown below is in a private collection.

Following demobilisation, Dupont studied for a further four years at the Royal Academy qualifying for the Diploma in the School of Painting. He was commissioned by the Dorsetshire Regiment to paint two pictures for the Officers' Mess, showing battles in which they had taken part during the Second World War. The two paintings that he produced 'Crossing the Rhine at Arnhem' and 'D-Day Landings' are now in the Keep Military Museum, Dorchester. Following the amalgamation in 1957 of the Dorsetshire Regiment with the Devonshire Regiment and a further amalgamation in 2007 with three other units to form 'The Rifles', the regimental collections of the Dorsetshire and Devonshire Regiments were put on display in the Keep Military Museum in Dorchester.

D-Day Landings   *Photo: The Keep Military Museum*

Crossing the Rhine at Arnhem   *Photo: The Keep Military Museum*

I have been able to piece together some aspects of Richard Dupont's post-war life from press cuttings. A report of the 1951 South Devon Hunt Ball showed a photograph of Dupont with three friends describes him as an artist who specialises in equestrian subjects.[4]

In 1952, the British horse Wilwyn, owned by Mr Robert Boucher of Teynham near Sittingbourne in Kent was the winner of the first International Washington DC race at Laurel Park, Maryland. When he sold the horse in 1960 to Harry Oppenheimer, a press report said that *'inside the house are ample reminders of Wilwyn....and a lovely painting of him by the famous Richard Dupont.'*[5]

At the South Devon Hunt Ball 1951
Richard Dupont is second from the left
Photo: Illustrated Sporting and Dramatic News

In 1956, Dupont painted a full-length study of Rustler, the stage and film star dog, whose bark and name became the trade mark of the 'Riders of the Range' stage and radio show. After the portrait had been unveiled, a NSPCC Inspector presented Rustler (official name Romulus of Whelan) with an out-size bone for services rendered to the Society.[6]

After painting equestrian subjects in America and Scandinavia, Dupont established a studio at Dedham in Essex where his neighbour was Sir Alfred Munnings, who was an inspiration to him at the Royal Academy. In 1944, Sir Alfred, then President of the Royal Academy, gave Dupont his first box and easel.

As well as painting horses Dupont rode them and was a member of the local Hunt.

Dupont received many equestrian commissions, including Hyperion and Alycidon for the Earl of Derby and Parthia and Alcide for Sir Humphrey de Trafford. Queen Elizabeth II commissioned him to paint her classic winners Aureole and Pall Mall and these pictures hang at Sandringham. In 1960, Dupont had a private interview with the Queen.

In 1959, Dupont was invited to paint in one of Munnings' studios in Dedham and in 1960 he had just opened a one man show in London, for which he had been working at one of the Munnings' studios in Dedham. Possibly Dupont was using the studio at Castle House soon after Munnings' death or he was using the Old Grammar school studio.[7]

In November 1960, Richard Dupont had his first exhibition depicting equestrian subjects at Messrs. Ackermann's Galleries in Old Bond Street. Some forty-seven paintings of horses, equestrian scenes and English country life were displayed. These were painted between commissions and showed his interest in the horse in rather more informal surroundings.[8]

Dupont moved to Torns Park in Ashburton, Devon in the late 1960s.

Torns Park in 2020

In 1971, the Cheshire Forest Hounds commissioned Richard Dupont to paint a portrait of Moses, the favourite horse of Philip Hunter MFH in recognition of 25 years' service as Master and Huntsman.[9]

In 1976, the Sir WW Wynn's Hunt held the preview of their Christmas exhibition depicting hunting scenes at Bickerton Institute. 'Away from Macefen' a painting by Richard Dupont was unveiled by the artist.[10]

Richard Dupont died on the 17 May 1977 at Torns Park and is buried at Widecombe-in-the-Moor in a grave of similar design to his parents. The inscription reads *Richard John Munro Dupont son of John Munro Dupont MD of Frome Somerset born: 20 July 1920 died 17 May 1977 equestrian and portrait painter British official War Artist World War II South East Asia Command.*

Dr and Mrs J M Dupont's grave
St John's churchyard, Frome
Photo: Cliff Howard

Richard Dupont's grave
Photo: Widecombe History Society

My research into Richard Dupont was started by seeing the picture below, painted by him and owned by Frome Museum, titled 'Pony Club Event'. This was given to the museum by Frome Town Council in 2013.

My researches have led to more questions than answers and, I think, that it was best summed up for me by a local historian in Ashburton who described him as 'the elusive Dupont'.

Thanks to David Dupont, Frome Museum, Ms Grainne Lenehan, Archivist, Marlborough College, Nick Speakman, Researcher, The Keep Military Museum, Dorchester, Bill Tetheredge, Curatorial Researcher at Munnings Art Museum, Dedham and Bob Heath, Trustee, Ashburton Museum.

References
[1] *9th (1843-1952) and 11th (1903-1996) editions of the Marlborough College Register.*
[2] *March on!: Infantry Battalions in England, India and Burma, 1941-1945 by Norman Havers. Square One Publications 1992*
[3] *Art. IWM ART LD 7550 - 7552*
[4] *Illustrated Sporting and Dramatic News 12 December 1951*
[5] *The East Kent Gazette 8 September 1961*
[6] *The Stage 20 December 1956*
[7] *Notes from Bob Tetheredge, Munnings Art Gallery*
[8] *Resumé produced to provide background for Dupont's exhibition at Messrs Ackermann's Galleries. Keep Military Museum, Dorchester M.D.R/DR/385/D*
[9] *Cheshire Observer 6 August 1971*
[10] *Cheshire Observer 3 December 1976*

Jesse Tucker (1890-1977) and Wilfred Harry Tucker (1887-1947)

Wilfred and Jesse Tucker were both born in Bradford-on-Avon to parents Harry and his wife Sarah (née Hannay). After Harry's death in 1902, Sarah and her family of seven surviving children moved to 6 Summer Hill in Frome where they lived for a number of years.

Jesse joined the 2nd Battalion of Prince Albert's Somersetshire Light Infantry in 1906, when he was only 15 years old. He wrote regularly to his older brother Wilfred from various postings near Plymouth, Malta and India where the 2nd Battalion spent the duration of the war. Wilfred joined the 3rd Battalion PASLI in 1907.

The photograph shows Jesse and Wilfred in the uniform of privates in the Somerset Light Infantry aged about 18 and 21 respectively. Interestingly their uniforms are slightly different indicating their separate regiments. They both survived the war and left Frome for Holmfirth in Yorkshire where the Tuckers had relatives.[1]

[1]*Catherine Hanley, The Weaver Family of Hemington and Frome, FSLS Yearbook 15, 2012*

I am indebted to Catherine Hanley for the photograph and information on Wilfred and Jesse Tucker. Ed

Hans Coper and Frome

Hans Coper was born in Chemnitz, near the German-Czech frontier in 1920, the son of a Jewish textile businessman, who committed suicide when Hans was 16, and a gentile mother; his family moved to Dresden after Hitler became *Reichskanzler*. Hans studied textile engineering, and, after hiding for six months in a hotel in Wiesbaden, emigrated to England in 1939, pawning his dress suit to pay for digs in Bloomsbury. After the declaration of war, he became 'an enemy alien' without possessions or security; he attempted to commit suicide but the gas ran out and he had no money for the meter. In 1940 he was arrested and sent to an internment camp in Lancashire and then to a concentration camp in Canada under freezing conditions. He eventually volunteered to join the Pioneer Corps and returned to England where he was posted to Salcombe in Devon where he dug trenches before transferring to Milborne Port, doing similar work. He became seriously ill, recovered and married his nurse.

Lucie Rie buttons

He continued various jobs as porter, mechanic and factory worker, while perfecting his drawing in the evenings. In 1943, he was introduced by William Ohly, who ran the Berkely Galleries to a Viennese refugee, Lucie Rie, a potter. This changed his fortunes; he began making hand pressed buttons for her, then domestic stoneware, cups and saucers under her creative supervision which developed into a lifelong collaboration. In the 1950s he was still making a basic living by working for Lucie but his work was exhibited in Amsterdam and the Berkely Gallery, and, in 1956 he had a small one-man show with his work reaching New York and Sweden. He separated from his partner of 10 years, Francesca, with whom he had two children, and moved to Bloomsbury where he lived alone in an austere flat.

In 1958, Hans had a solo show at Primavera in Sloane Street, which was a major success after which he was offered a studio at Digswell House in Welwyn Garden City by Henry Morris. He lived there for five years producing 'some of the most forceful and striking work of his career.' This formed the Rothschild Collection which was later acquired by York Museum for their Centre of Ceramic Art. Meanwhile he had met Jane Gate, a photography student at the London School of Printing, who made a photographic record of his work over the next 25 years. In 1962 Basil Spence commissioned him to make monumental candlesticks for the rebuilt Coventry Cathedral, part of his 'architectural phase.'

From the left: Lucie Rie, Hans Coper and Jane Gate
Photo: Courtesy Crafts Magazine[1]

Hans' career was improving; he taught at the Camberwell School of Art and continued to teach at the Royal College of Art until 1975. He had moved his studio to an outbuilding in Hammersmith belonging to Jane's uncle in 1963 and had another one man show at the Berkely Gallery in 1965. Prices for his ceramics were improving and Lucie Rie helped Hans buy a house in a blighted road which was reprieved and he was able to sell it and search for a new home. In 1967, Hans and Jane bought a derelict farmhouse in Spring Gardens, Cherry Tree Farm to which Hans had originally said: 'No! Never!' on first sight. They were married in 1974 but Hans was diagnosed with motor-neurone disease a year later, after which he rarely left the house and workshop. He continued to make pots under increasing difficulty until 1979 with the final firing of the kiln in 1980; he died in June 1981.

Cherry Tree Farm
Photo: Paul Payne

The candlesticks commissioned for the rebuilt Coventry Cathedral in 1962
Photo: Julian Osley

During the early 1970s Michael and Eileen Sellers had created the Selwood Gallery in the old White Swan in Vallis Road; there were 14 pots by Hans Coper at the grand opening at prices ranging from £28 to £46. A special area, Hans' Corner, was given over to the sale of his pots and over a period of four years about thirty were sold. Writing for the Antiques Collector in 1976, Michael highlighted the importance of the sale of one of Hans' pots by Sotheby's as 'the professional and public recognition of a great artist.' The Copers and Sellers became friends and Hans explained to Michael some of his special techniques such as putting oboe nails to reinforce the apex of the pots where they reduced to a very fine point.

The Hans Coper collection showing a potters wheel made by Hans Coper
Photo: Estate of Hans Coper/York Museum Trust

During the 1980s there was increased interest in 20th century ceramics which was driven by the major auction houses, particularly influenced by a former film director, Cyril Frankel, who had become Bonham's ceramics expert. Sotheby's staged a 'Hans Up' sale and thereafter prices always topped four figures. In 1980 an early thistle pot by Hans sold for £8,000 which was 'by far the highest sum paid for a work by a living potter,' however, this was soon surpassed by another Coper; in due course his work went on to fetch a record £305,000 for a vase in a sale in Exeter in 2018. In 1987 the Post Office commissioned a series of four stamps featuring the work of British potters including Hans Coper and Lucie Rie.

When the Copers bought the derelict Cherry Tree Farm, they had very little money, so Hans used his versatility to design, mend and make do: he planned a new lean-to extension to the converted byre which he used as a studio, designed the most original wood burner and a special chimney cowl that he made to avoid it smoking. They created a superb garden where Jane kept goats. This started in 1972 with 'Jennea', a goat from Writhlington School that became famous. In exchange Hans made a large pot 78 cm tall which he gave to the school; it used to be at the entrance of the old building where it served

The vase which sold for a record £305,000 in Exeter in 2018
Photo: Bearnes, Hampton & Littlewood

50

as an umbrella stand until the school was fund raising for a new sports centre in 1996, when it was sold by Sotheby's at auction for £30,000. Other beneficiaries of Hans' art were neighbours, Doreen and Ted Appleby who lived opposite and shared an interest with Jane in weaving. They admired Hans' and Lucie's work and formed a collection over the years which was later sold at Bonhams.

After Hans had died Jane continued to live at Cherry Tree Farm until 1995 when it was bought by Lin and Brian Walton who appreciated the legacy of the building and its association with the Copers: the bedroom that Hans had designed for his daughter, Anya, who had lived there for some time and the platform in the living room, where Jane had her spinning wheel and loom, which had served for many of the photographs of Hans' pots.

By the time the Copers came to Frome, Hans' health was already affected and became worse after the diagnosis of motor-neurone disease. In the past he had been known for his 'quiet self-deprecating wit, his love of coffee, beer, whisky, poker and, especially, his love of parties; he clearly got great benefit and warmth from the close company of friends.' During his last years he suffered severely from his illness which was so frustrating but although reclusive, he always remained very polite and kind, and very interested in other people. Indeed, constant politeness was one of the things that even casual friends remember best about Hans.

The Writhlington School vase
Photo: Sotheby's

He and Jane lived in Spring Gardens for the last 14 years of his life, a man who has been recognised as: 'the most important and respected potter of the 20th century.'

This article was made possible by the generosity of Paul Payne[2] and the unpublished research of Mandy Bloom[3] for the forthcoming book 'Hans Connections: The interwoven local lives touched by Hans and Jane Coper, and Lucie Rie'. In addition, thanks are due to Stenlake Publishing for permission to quote from Hans Coper by Tony Birks[4]. Ed

[1]*Crafts Magazine,The Crafts Council, www.craftscouncil.org.uk*
[2]*Paul Payne, www.porcelainlights.co.uk*
[3]*Mandy Bloom Memoirs, www.mandybloom.co.uk*
[4]*Tony Birks, Hans Coper, Stenlake Publishing, 2013, www.stenlake.co.uk*

JOHN SINKINS 1805 – 1869
by Margery Hyde

John Sinkins in 1867

John Sinkins was the son of Jane (née Hine) and James Sinkins (1774 – 1811). James Sinkins was the only surviving son of John Sinkins (17?? – 1805) a draper in Frome with a shop in the Upper Market Place. John Sinkins Sr married twice; his first wife, Rachel Wilcox of Berkley, gave him two sons but died shortly after the birth of the second son who predeceased her. Three months later John Sinkins Sr was remarried to Sarah Clace of Rodden who was a milliner. In October 1804, his son, James, married Jane Hine (1783 – 1864)[1] in Beaminster, Dorset. Although, at his marriage, James Sinkins is described as a draper there was clearly more to the family business than just the shop. His father, John Sinkins Sr, owned or leased several properties in the town and, at his death in 1805 left both the shop and a substantial property portfolio to his only son.

The marriage of James and Jane produced a son (John) and two daughters (Jane and Ann) but James Sinkins, died in June 1811. Ann Sinkins, their daughter died in 1825 aged fifteen. The family initially lived in Cheap Street with James' stepmother and the shop was located in the Market Place at what is now the site of HSBC Bank. After the death of her husband, Jane Sinkins was left with the three small children and the business which was held in trust for her son. Jane herself proved to be socially ambitious and, after transferring the shop to her son when he married, moved home to 7, South Parade which was considered a more desirable address than central Frome. By 1844 she had left her shopkeeping days behind her and, in Pigot's Directory of that year[2], is listed among the gentry of Frome.

Before this rise in status, the business flourished under the title of Jane Sinkins & Son and it would appear that Mrs Sinkins was a force to be reckoned with. In 1818 the town constable, Isaac Gregory[3], records that Mrs Sinkins had complained that a standing post had been placed in front of her door and prevented its use. Mr Gregory got help and removed the post but the market bailiff then censured him for interfering and removing Lord Cork's property. Lord Cork owned the market rights and the lease to the Sinkins shop, however, there is no record that the post was moved back suggesting that both bailiff and constable feared the wrath of Mrs Sinkins more than that of Lord Cork.

The Hine family seem to have been natural entrepreneurs, active in business and the professions. Jane was the second youngest of eleven children and her siblings could be found in London, Nottingham, France and Canada as well as closer to home in Dorset and Somerset. John Sinkins was later able to call upon family members whenever he sought advice or a service.

Jane Sinkins is buried in the Dissenters' Cemetery and there is a plaque[1] to her memory on the wall of the former Zion Chapel in Whittox Lane.

John Sinkins was born in 1805 and in 1830 he married Eliza Stancomb of Trowbridge the daughter of a wealthy mill owner. The business in the Market Place was made over to him that year but there is no record that he worked there himself. The marriage produced three daughters and a son. His middle daughter, Elizabeth (Bessie), went on to marry Philip Le Gros, the owner of the silk mill in Merchants' Barton. His son, William, became a cavalry officer and married Selina Senior of Hampshire. The oldest daughter, Margaret married John Bayfield Clark, a wool manufacturer of Wingfield and his youngest daughter, Jane, remained single and is recorded as living at Welshmill House until her death in 1915.

Initially, the family lived at Vallis House, close to Hapsford Mill, but Sinkins very soon purchased Wallbridge House which he then extended thus adding new rooms to a total of

ten bedrooms. A watercolour by one of the family in Frome Museum shows the interior of the drawing room suggesting a comfortable environment for the family. They maintained at least five servants, stables and a carriage and their social life went beyond Frome. The daughters went to school in London and Thomas Green's diaries[4] show that there were family visits to them during term time.

Wallbridge House

The Sinkins family drawing room in Wallbridge House

They frequently visited relations elsewhere in the country and had the extended family to stay. The discomfort of travel whether by coach or by train seems to have been no deterrent to their sociability or hospitality.

While recognised as an astute businessman, John Sinkins was also known for his generosity. He was a supporter of the life of Frome and gave to many causes. Wallbridge House came with a substantial amount of land and again, Sinkins was generous toward the town. Each year, the meadow at the back of the house was made available, at no cost, to the Frome Agricultural Association for their exhibition and show. He was on the committee of the Frome Agricultural Association and donated a prize of £1.0.0 for the grower of the twelve best swede turnips and later the prize for the twelve best mangel-wurzels. The meadow was also made available to other Frome Societies including the Frome Selwood Cricket Club, Frome Athletics Club and the Band of Hope.

At a later date, Sinkins was able to sell a large parcel of land at the front of the house to the Great Western Railway Company. The opening of the Frome Station in 1850, was celebrated with a large dinner at the Crown Hotel over which John Sinkins presided and made a speech.

John Sinkins gave to the town in both time and money. He was on the committee to establish the Frome Market Hall. He chaired the Committees of the Fire and Life Assurance Society and was a director of the Frome Selwood Mutual Benefit Society. He was an Ensign in the Frome Volunteer Rifles and a trustee of the Frome Penny Bank. He was also Chairman of the Vestry Committee (parish council). Both he and Thomas Green, his brother-in-law, were involved with the establishment of the Frome Literary and Scientific Institution and he continued that involvement until his death.

John Sinkins' sister, Jane, married their cousin Thomas Green, the son of a Nottingham lace manufacturer. Thomas Green, who had his own business interests, became his main adviser and accountant, the two men working closely together. It was on Green's advice that John Sinkins went into partnership with Levi Wood of Great Elm thus establishing the company of Wood & Sinkins. The business was based at Hapsford Mill but later expanded and moved to Stapleford Mill. The partnership was dissolved in 1869 shortly before John Sinkins died and Levi Wood carried on as the sole owner.

Sinkins and Wood made cloth for livery coats for the servants of the aristocracy and for the linings of carriages.

In the manufacture of livery cloths Messrs Sinkins & Wood have to be very careful in preserving the old tints of colour, which have become hereditary pride of many noble families in the liveries of their servants: the faintest change would be discarded as being almost an infringement upon their ancient dignity.[5]

Although, by then, the wool trade in Frome had declined, Sinkins and Wood were sufficiently specialist to have remained in business and to continue to flourish. It seems that Levi Wood was the active partner involved in the day-to-day running of the mill. John Sinkins was a sleeping partner with an active interest in the finances. Thomas Green's diaries[4] record that both he and John Sinkins would visit the mill regularly but there is no record of daily attendance or any significant involvement in the management of the business.

John Sinkins prospered; he continued to own the shop in the Market Place but did not work there himself. Instead he employed managers including his own cousin William Hine May who went into partnership with him and ran the shop until 1854 when the partnership was dissolved. He was also noted for his many acts of kindness to individuals. Alfred Rowland, the minister of Zion, records:

One of the richest men in my congregation, John Sinkins, JP, was a typical squire in appearance, and bluff, tender-hearted, yet boisterous in manner. He had in his stables a high-spirited Irish mare with a villainous temper. She really belonged to his son, an officer in the Guards, but as he was rarely at home, she had very little exercise. Mr Sinkins, in a fit of good-nature, offered the use of the mare to me, and, rather to his surprise I think, I gratefully accepted the offer, and took her out, generally on a Monday morning, for two or three hours.[6]

He was a staunch supporter of Zion Chapel and a constant attender there to the end of his life. His father, James, had represented the Zion trustees in the negotiations for the purchase of the land and the family connection remained. James' widow, son and daughter continued in their loyalty to Zion Chapel. However, John Sinkins' wife, Eliza, preferred to worship at Holy Trinity Church. Her daughter, Margaret was married there and both Eliza Sinkins and her unmarried daughter, Jane are buried there. Her other daughter, Bessie also married at Holy Trinity but worshipped at Zion Chapel and is buried in the Dissenters

Cemetery. John Sinkins is buried in the Dissenters Cemetery in the same grave as his mother, sister and brother-in-law.

John Sinkins was made a Justice of the Peace and, as a magistrate, seems to have practised benevolence. It is recorded that he often paid the fines himself rather than let a poor man go to prison through poverty. However, he didn't always maintain the impartiality that the law requires. In 1860 the murder of Savile Kent at Road Hill to which his half-sister, Constance, pleaded guilty, became a national sensation. In the early stages of the case, John Sinkins was one of the magistrates hearing the cases against two individuals, each accused of the murder. In July 1860 the *Taunton Courier* published a letter from Sinkins giving his opinion of the murder as:

> *That the deed was done by an individual far too intimately acquainted with him (the victim) there cannot be a shadow of doubt.*[7]

Today this lack of neutrality would probably see him removed from the bench, or, at least sent for re-training.

The lasting legacy of his generosity is the building that housed the Frome Literary and Scientific Institution which had been founded in 1844 with Thomas Bunn as its first secretary. Both John Sinkins and Thomas Green were on the committee that were to struggle to find suitable premises. It had started in Palmer Street but Thomas Green's diary records that committee meetings and lectures took place in The George Hotel which suggests that Palmer Street was unsuitable for public use although it housed a newsroom and library for the members to use. Eventually John Sinkins came to the rescue and donated both the land and a new building to the town with no intention of reaping a profit. The architect was James Hine, the son of John Sinkins' cousin, Thomas. James Hine had a practice in Plymouth and was responsible for the design of many of the public buildings (Town Hall, Guildhall, schools and chapels) in the city. As such he was a noted architect but, sadly, many of these buildings were demolished by bombs during the Second World War. The Frome building was completed in 1869 and was in use by February of that year. The *Frome Times* records:

The history of the Institution is a record of steady and safe progress. Established in 1844, it has afforded a kind of neutral meeting-ground for literary and scientific discussion, as well as a resting place for a valuable library and one of the richest and most varied museums of which any country town can boast. As is well known its habitation until now in Palmer Street, where its collection had but little chance of being seen with advantage. Through the large-hearted liberality of Mr Sinkins, however, the Institution has now a suite of spacious rooms – a building which is not only an adornment to the town, but which is in every respect calculated to carry out the generous intention of its founder.[8]

The opening was deferred because of John Sinkins' unexpectedly early death on 24 November that year. This building now houses Frome Museum. The death was felt to be one of public loss. The Local Board resolved:

That in consideration of the esteem generally felt for the late John Sinkins Esq. This Board resolves that the members pay a last tribute to the memory of their colleague by attending his funeral; and suggests that those of their fellow townsmen who share their feeling and wish to join the procession should meet them at Wallbridge on Friday next, the 3 December, at quarter past two o'clock punctually.[9]

As a result of this other groups in the town passed similar resolutions and joined the funeral procession to the Dissenters Cemetery. Many of the shops closed and along the funeral route residents drew the blinds on their windows as a mark of respect. The *Salisbury and Wiltshire Times* records:

On Friday afternoon the mortal remains of our lamented townsman, Mr John Sinkins were laid in their final resting place in the cemetery in the presence of such a concourse of people as has seldom been gathered together on a like occasion. The family of the deceased gentleman having consented to the desire of the townspeople to join in the funeral procession, notices were issued to that effect. The funeral cortege was, therefore, very imposing and spread over nearly half-a-mile of the distance from Wallbridge House to the cemetery.

There follows a list of those bodies represented in the procession and it finishes with:

All along the route, upwards of a mile and a half, the streets were lined with spectators, but the management was so excellent, that no confusion or stoppage took place. The first portion of the burial service was read at Wallbridge House by the Rev A Daniel, Vicar of Holy Trinity, and at the cemetery, which is a strictly Noncomformist burial-place, the Rev A Rowland, of Zion Chapel, concluded the service, offered an impressive prayer, and the sad ceremony terminated.[10]

John Sinkins' widow, Eliza lived on until 1892. Their son, William Stancomb, known as Stancomb, married but there were no children to carry on the surname of this branch of the Sinkins family in Frome. A plaque to John Sinkins was placed in Zion Chapel but can no longer be traced.

[1]*Margery Hyde, Jane Sinkins 1782-1864, FSLS Yearbook 19, 2016*
[2]*Pigot's Directory for Frome and surrounding Villages, 1844*
[3]*Michael McGarvie, Crime and Punishment in Regency Frome, FSLS, 1984*
[4]*Thomas Green, Diaries 1840-1845*
[5]*Samuel Cuzner, Hand-Book to Froome-Selwood, 1866*
[6]*Alfred Rowland, An independent Parson, Congregational Union, 1923*
[7]*Taunton Courier, 18 July 1860*
[8]*Frome Times, 10 February1869*
[9]*Somerset and Wiltshire Courier, 14 December 1869*
[10]*Salisbury and Wiltshire Times 11 December 1869*

FROME BUILDINGS No 23

Wallington & Weston

Houston's cloth mill in Vallis Way was founded in the late 18th century and was rebuilt in 1866. It continued to operate as Henry Houston and Sons until 1945. Wallington and Weston who were manufacturing rubber goods at St John's Mill, Adderwell moved to Vallis Way in 1946 then forming Frome Plastics Limited. This company was taken over by the Marley Tile Co to make flooring products which ceased in 1979 and the Wallington and Weston division was sold to ICI Hyde Plastics. The plant closed finally in 2003 and the site has now been replaced by housing.

My thanks to Michael McGarvie for this aerial photograph which dates from about 1950 and shows the original mill buildings to the east. Ed

William Brett Harvey-A Busy Man*

by Nick Hersey

Individuals can make a difference: Genghis Khan, Winston Churchill, Rosa Parks. Less dramatically, the impact of one man on a 'decaying town in the West' is the subject of this article.[1] It will deal with the temperance movement, Nonconformism and the shaping of the working class. All of these things would have existed in Frome, 'the plucky little borough,' if he had not, but he undoubtedly made a difference as to how they developed,[2] which is not to say he was the only driving force, but he was the most effective and the longest lived.

Nineteenth century Britain saw many moral and political crusades, for example: Chartism, the Anti-Corn Law League and of course the anti-slavery movement. This latter certainly had much support in Frome by 1825, judging from a poster showing such well-known Fromian surnames such as Wickham, Sheppard and Bunn.[3] From the 1830s onwards, nationally and in Frome, another such crusade was the temperance movement. Initially this word of moderation meant a personal commitment to avoid spirits and be cautious concerning any consumption of alcohol. Soon, however, the word became used to mean a personal commitment to abstain from alcohol and often to support legal measures to prohibit the sale or production of alcohol.

In the southwest, the temperance movement seems to have started in Bristol in 1830, and societies were formed in Bath and Chippenham in 1832.[4] The first temperance organisation in Frome began in 1834, although Fromians John Sheppard and Rev Dyer were speaking at temperance meetings in 1832 and 1833.[5] However this Fromian anti-spirits movement collapsed in acrimony in 1835 and was replaced by a total abstinence organisation in 1836.[6]

* Abbreviations are shown on page 69. Ed

For two decades the leading figures in the movement were Samuel Horton, a grocer, and Joseph Chapman jr, a master mason. The early 1840s have many optimistic reports from Frome district. There are positive accounts of Horton and Chapman's lectures, burgeoning societies in neighbouring villages such as Nunney and Road and numerous 'respectable' meetings, galas and parades.[7] Nonetheless Fromian temperance at this stage, as Horton reports, is largely characterised by its 'long silence' because 'the harvest truly is great, but the labourers are few'.[8] Then in 1855 William Brett Harvey (WBH) arrived in Frome.

WBH was born in Great Surrey Street (now Blackfriars Road) in London on 3 October 1830. His parents, George and Caroline née Bewsey had married in Caroline's home parish of Horsington in 1828 and WBH, the middle of three brothers, was baptised at the Independent Chapel at Union Street, Southwark on 20 March 1831.[9] His father, a chemist and druggist, appears in London Post Office directories from 1825 at 63 Great Surrey Street. In early 1839 George sold his business to Oliver Springett Iron and in February 1839 was recorded in the London Gazette as offering to purchase all the saleable assets of the bankrupt James Sellers, Druggist, of Yeovil.[10] Ironically George Harvey of Yeovil, 'chymist,' was the petitioning creditor in the subsequent bankruptcy of Oliver Springett Iron.[11]

The dates are important here since it seems most likely that the Harveys were in Yeovil for several months before Rev John Jukes departed for Bedford and that George's chemist's shop was 2 minutes walk from John Jukes' chapel in Princes Street. This then was where WBH met Eliza Marsh Jukes, whom he married in Bedford in 1857.[12] However the first key episode in WBH's life was on 16 September 1842, when he signed the teetotal pledge in the house of Rev W Robinson.[13] This was a brave act for a youth of twelve, given the persecution of teetotallers that was common at that date.[14] Some time after that he began training in earnest for life as a pharmaceutical chemist holding responsible positions in Southampton, Bristol and London, finally qualifying in 1868.[15] He was living in Bristol, with his parents in 1851 and Frome's Zion Chapel records show his official transfer from an unnamed Bristol chapel in January 1856.[16] Was it only coincidence that he chose to move to Frome, boyhood home of Rev John Jukes, his future father-in-law? Was it coincidence that, of all the options, he chose to join Zion Chapel, John Jukes' boyhood chapel, and become involved in the Sunday School which fifty years earlier hosted John Jukes as one of its first scholars, and afterwards as a teacher?[17] Clearly there is a life plan here, but no personal details have yet been discovered, any more than has the source of the money with which he purchased William Langford's pharmacy and bookshop at 20 Bath Street, Frome in December 1855. As part of this deal, he also purchased the *Somerset and Wilts Journal (SWJ)*, then the only local paper in Frome which claimed a weekly circulation of 1,000.[18] Ownership of the *SWJ* was key to the implementation of WBH's vision and he swiftly tripled its circulation to 3000.[19] He was not just the owner, he was the editor. He did employ staff, and in the early years he contracted out the printing to W T Butler but from the beginning he exercised a close control, particularly over editorial content.[20] Through this we can learn much about WBH's views, and, at times, this article depends greatly on *SWJ* editorials and reports.

WBH's faith was at the core of his being. In Yeovil his parents were closely involved in the church, his mother being Superintendent of the Congregational Girls' School where his father was also a teacher. His parents' influence meant WBH also attended the Sunday school and in later years he would say that 'he owed his conversion to his mother's prayers'. He also credited, 'the teaching and influence of his parents, who were missionary enthusiasts' with his own 'interest in the great missionary cause'.[21] Given the effect that his formative years had on him, it is not surprising that WBH began Sunday school teaching himself in 1848 and was still involved in 1914.[22] As Superintendent of Zion Chapel Sunday School, he seems to be speaking from a conviction born of personal experience when he tells parents 'their children would be pretty much what they made them. They were responsible for the habits they formed, the training of their minds and the formation of their characters. Let them try to instruct their children in God's word, and pray with and for their children'.[23]

Family was important: hence, whilst this article is largely about WBH's public life, WBH the family man should not be forgotten. In the fourteen years they were married, WBH and Eliza Marsh Jukes had six children, Eliza dying from anaemia, childbirth and exhaustion after the birth of their last child[24]. The sole boy, William Jukes Harvey, died suddenly, from 'a visitation of God,' aged only six months in 1865, while the oldest daughter, Mary Caroline who married Arthur Henry Coombs, died soon after the birth of a stillborn son in 1888[25], however neither death nor Arthur's subsequent remarriage nor ordination as a Baptist minister could separate the men. Arthur and his new wife gave a wedding present at Florence Harvey's wedding in 1892 and Arthur received a legacy of £2 in WBH's will. It was he who wrote WBH's obituary in the *SWJ* in 1918[26].

The youngest daughter, Lizzie Marsh Jukes never married and lived with her father. An able Sunday school student, the adult Lizzie was involved in the Zion Mother's Meeting and the Naish's Street Mission. She was local secretary for the British Society for the Propagation of the Gospel among the Jews and treasurer of the Frome branch of the British Women's Temperance Association. She ran stalls in fund-raising events and sang in both chapel and temperance events often also dueting with her father.[27] She died in 1938 and probate was granted to Eric Walter Harvey Vallis.[28]

Annie Eliza, who married Rowland Hibberd in 1890, left Frome but remained in contact with the family, attending her sister Florence's wedding in 1892 and her father's 80th birthday celebration in 1910. The report of their wedding showed that WBH was still in contact with the Jukes and the Bewseys, both related to his late wife. Rowland outlived Annie, but when he died in 1946 one of his executors was Eric Walter Harvey Vallis.[29]

WBH and Mr and Mrs WH Penny had known each other for many years before their children married. They were members of the same church and Mrs Penny often sang or played the piano in church or temperance musical events.[30] They also supported some of the same worthy causes, such as the Frome Mutual Benefit Building Society and the British and Foreign Bible Society,[31] hence it seems clear how their children met. Francis Harry Penny and Louisa Griffith Harvey married in August 1889.[32] FH Penny was very involved in community activities: he actively campaigned to improve flood defences for the market place, was honorary secretary of the Sunday School Union, participated in temperance entertainments and served, with WBH, on the Urban District Council.[33] Unfortunately he and Louisa had to join FH Penny's brother in Mexico after FH Penny was declared bankrupt in 1906.[34] He died there 'while in the prime of life'.[35] Louisa and their only child Francis William Mervyn came back by themselves for WBH's 80th birthday, landing at Plymouth in September 1910, before returning to Mexico.[36] They arrived at Falmouth from Kingston Jamaica, again without Francis, in January 1915, and gave Dunmore, WBH's house, as their address.[37] She died in 1938 and probate was granted to Eric Walter Harvey Vallis.[38]

Finally in 1892, Florence Elizabeth Harvey married Lewis Walter Vallis, a farmer from Hemington who was one of the founders of the Hemington BOH in 1877.[39] Again the families had known each other for some time, LW Vallis presenting the 1882 annual report at a temperance meeting at Faulkland where WBH gave a speech. By 1890 Lewis was close enough to the Harveys to be mentioned in the report of the Harvey/Hibberd wedding. WBH would also have known WC Vallis, Lewis' father, who was on the Board of Guardians. WBH and LW Vallis served on the Board of Guardians together in the early 1900s and often worked together on temperance matters.[40]

The pattern is consistent across the Harvey family and those families with whom they intermarried: clear Christian faith, a commitment to the temperance movement, involvement in the community and Liberal politics.[41]

For WBH himself, it should also be remembered, as Rev Alfred Shave said at his funeral, that he had 'the gift of music'.[42] He was not the only such talented person in Frome: JD Cox, for example, was a similarly able organiser and performer.[43] Indeed in those pre-broadcasting and pre-gramophone days, music seems to have been a major form of entertainment in Frome. On Christmas Eve 1861, for example, several parties of singers, hand-bell ringers and three bands were to 'send forth sweet strains of harmony' on Frome's streets into Christmas Day.[44] More ambitiously, WBH sang and played harmonium in JD Cox's production of Handel's Messiah in 1867, while in 1882 the *Frome Times* said of a production of Haydn's Creation: 'With Mr W B Harvey as conductor it will readily be understood that the oratorio was given in a manner worthy the genius of the great composer.'[45] He was still gaining applause for his singing in a production of the Messiah in 1906, however he was just as happy singing a few songs at a friendly society meeting or dueting with his daughter at a village temperance meeting if that was what was needed.[46]

In his religious work WBH also sang and played but here he often did so to a higher purpose. Music in support of Christian goals, such as at a Zion Christian Band musical evening, was one thing, but Church music itself was another. In a service, he insisted, music must be 'intensely devotional,' an integral part of the worship and not merely attractive.[47] If necessary, he was happy to take a backseat role, simply 'accompanying... on the harmonium,' but he was a 'talented conductor' of the Sunday School Union, the Temperance Choir and the Free Church Choral Union and still 'delighted all present' with his singing in 1914.[48] At Zion Chapel, he was organist and leader of the choir and, although he had by then retired from these leadership roles, 'on the Sunday before his death he occupied his usual place in the choir'.[49]

As a background to his temperance work and religious activities, it is important to remember the business activity that allowed WBH to maintain himself and his family. Today one would not expect to meet someone who was a bookseller, printer, publisher and pharmaceutical chemist but a combination of different occupations was a much more common way of earning a living in the 19th century. WBH was a true entrepreneur, selling the popular perfumes and patent medicines of the day but also using his knowledge to make his own preparations, such as The Frome Selwood Bouquet, Harvey's Pectoral Elixir and Harvey's Nursery Hair Lotion (for head-lice).[50] However his most successful product seems to have been Harvey's Bilious and Liver Pills, which he manufactured for sixty years. In the 1860s he claimed over sixty local agents for these pills across the country, mostly in the South West, but also four in London and five in Manchester. Whilst in business he regularly published testimonials from satisfied customers and took this product into retirement, selling his pills from home. The edition of the *SWJ* that announced his death also contained the regular advertisement for 'Harvey's Bilious and Liver Pills'.[51]

WBH would sell anything that he thought would turn a profit, for example, his extensive Christmas range of annuals.[52] At one stage he was even Frome agent for *The Osprey*, which sailed regularly from Bristol to Quebec: perhaps this was why he sold 'Strong Iron-Bound Chests, suitable for sea-voyages.[53] In the 1880s he was an agent for the General Insurance Company.[54] However he also sold many items that supported his personal beliefs and interests, such as political publications and a range of Church Services and Prayer Books.[55] In 1886 an advertisement describes his shop as the local depot for the Religious Tract Society

---

PROTECTION TO THE LUNGS.

W. B. HARVEY

Would invite attention to his extensive stock of

RESPIRATORS,

Ranging in price from 1s. to 28s.

LUNG PROTECTORS,

Which effectually protect the Respiratory Organs from cold, by covering the Chest, both front and back, fitting up close to the nape of the neck.

CHEST PROTECTORS

In Felt, Chamois, and Hare Skin.

An assortment will be sent on approval if required.

W. B. HARVEY, Pharmaceutical Chemist, Frome.

EFFERVESCENT

SALINE

Will be found eminently useful as a Cooling and Antibilious agent.

It is a much more elegant Preparation than the old Seidlitz or Soda Powders, and by its means a pleasant, cooling, and refreshing draught can be obtained at any time, with little cost or trouble. Its value in Sick Headache, Nausea, Heartburn, and similar affections is generally admitted, and experience has proved it to be one of the best household remedies.

1s. 6d. per Bottle, same size as other similar Preparations sold at 2s. 9d.

SOLD BY

W. B. HARVEY,

PHARMACEUTICAL CHEMIST,

20, BATH STREET, FROME.

Advertisement 1860s

63

Library. Trade directories additionally record him as the local depository for The British and Foreign Bible Society, The Church of England Sunday School Institute, The Sunday School Union and National Temperance.[56] Given his involvement in various choirs, it is not surprising that he sold music.[57] His temperance beliefs led him to manufacture non-alcoholic beverages for winter and summer and, as an experienced businessman, he knew the advantages of offering discounts for large purchases or cash as well as to worthy but impoverished schools and charitable causes.[58]

Obviously making a profit was important, but on the other hand WBH never charged the local BOH for any of its numerous advertisements and, on at least one occasion, when he sold hymn books the church received 13% of the value of the sales.[59] In a similar vein, WBH declined the allowance to which he was entitled as Zion Chapel organist. Indeed, when his co-religionists were planning a presentation to thank him for his services, Rev FW Clarke said that they knew they could not just present him with the money collected because 'in that case he would simply give half of it away'.[60] There is a warmth in Clarke's words to 'Dear Mr Harvey' which does seem to reflect the respect and indeed love in which WBH was generally, though not universally, held.[61]

In the course of more than sixty years' residence in Frome, how did WBH go from being a new arrival, to the head of a 'well-known and much respected' family to Frome's 'Grand Old Man,' a description which, as a committed Gladstonian, it seems likely he would have enjoyed?[62] His generosity has already been touched upon. It was usual for a man in WBH's position to appear on public subscription lists, and WBH was no exception donating to the Frome auxiliary of the Bible Society, the Mechanics Institute's 'New Building Fund,' the fund to assist jeweller Henry Webb recover from a robbery, the fund to purchase a new horse for Police Superintendent Deggan and the local British Schools amongst many others.[63] He was also the sort of man who would put his hand in his pocket during a worthy whip-round or fund a prize to reward youthful endeavour or achievement,[64] but more importantly, WBH gave his energy and his time freely to causes and organisations.

One of the earliest organisations that WBH chose to support was the Mechanics Institute, the *SWJ* saying 'we very cordially commend this institution to the support of our readers'. WBH was on the organising committee by July 1857 and had been elected a trustee of the new Mechanics Hall by 1858. His decision, due to pressure of time, to resign the former position in 1860 was very much regretted since he had been 'so useful' in the mass of work needed to book speakers.[65] WBH saw the Mechanics Institute as a useful organisation to 'wean the working man from the beer house,' and, despite declining to rejoin the committee when elected, played a leading part in the successful penny readings programme of the mid-1860s.[66] Unfortunately, attempts to 'raise the character of the readings,' failed to impress and Frome's Mechanics Institute suffered declining numbers. 'First-class lecturers failed to draw an audience' or only attracted the middle-classes and reports of WBH's involvement ceased in the early 1870s, by which time he was deeply involved in temperance work.[67]

The Mechanics Institute building

'Give me a child until he is seven and I will show you the man,' is an idea widely attributed to both Ignatius Loyola and Aristotle and obviously in accord with how WBH believed he had been shaped by his parents. By the middle of the 19th century, British temperance activists were also coming to the conclusion that 'it would be far more effective to raise abstainers from childhood' than it would be to challenge adult habits, hence Clara Balfour's assertion in 1857: 'Give me the children, and I care not who has the men and women'.[68] BOHs, the *SWJ* reported, were to be established: 'to place a barrier between the current and the next generation'. Children who took the BOH pledge had 'secured themselves' against the evil habits surrounding them.[69] This was why WBH set about the creation of a BOH in Frome.

There was nothing new about this idea. Western Temperance League conferences had been endorsing the youth movement concept since at least 1844 and articles and advertisements concerning BOHs appeared regularly in the *WTH*.[70] As with other teetotal organisations, BOH members pledged a lifetime's abstinence from alcohol but BOHs were aimed at children who at that time were almost as likely to be consuming alcohol as adults.[71] However the Frome BOH was unusual in that it soon included adults as members, not just as organisers: its full title, from 1859, being the Band of Hope and Abstainers' Union.[72] Some writers report that temperance organisations were working-class, self-help movements, and this seems plausible in Northern England.[73] Such was not the case in Frome. The inaugural meeting heard WBH's pre-prepared 'plan of operations' and plea for 'pecuniary assistance'. Together with the Rev Manning's resolution 'nominating three ladies and three gentlemen to form a committee,' it is clear that Frome's organisation was to be very much in the paternalistic Fromian tradition of the middle-classes doing good to the poor.[74] A subsequent meeting of the committee with various Dissenting ministers to confer 'as to the most desirable method of constituting the society' only confirms this impression, as does the appointment as co-secretaries of the society of WBH and Mr MJ Bailey, a British Schools' teacher.[75] Support amongst the nonconformist community was widespread: the lack of Church of England involvement in the first decades is striking.

From its earliest days, the Christian influence on the Frome BOH can also be seen in the way it was organised. Dissenting chapels, as a matter of course, kept an eye on their members, punishing drunkenness and moral turpitude.[76] By the end of 1844, Zion Chapel had decided to follow the model already in operation at Badcox Lane Chapel 'by which the town is divided into districts, & each district placed under the charge of one of the Deacons, whose duty it is to watch over, advise with & assist the church members resident in his district'.[77] This methodology actually mirrored that of the Visiting Society of 1832 so it is not surprising to read that, at its foundation, the Frome BOH divided the town into districts 'by which organisation a constant supervision of the members is kept up'.[78] The oversight in each district was the responsibility of 'some of the elder youths', a male secretary and a female visitor being assigned to each. The secretary's responsibility was to return the membership cards which were collected at meetings, as a way of monitoring attendance, and to sell the *BOHR*. The visitor's task was to visit those who had missed meetings, 'as we think absence indicates a declension of interest,' and to report to her secretary.

In 1860 Frome's BOH was considered to be 'in a highly organised and complete state' and was being cited, nationally, as an example of how a local organisation should be conducted. WBH made it quite clear that it was the ladies and gentlemen of the committee who were in charge and that they were elected by 'Subscribers' and not members. By this stage two young men were appointed as Superintendents, their task being to be 'the medium of communication between the Committee and the District Secretaries'. With the apparent abolition of the role of visitor, the District Secretaries were tasked with visiting 'all the members at least once a month' and making 'a record of the steadfastness or otherwise of each member, comprising the reason where they have violated their pledge'. As well as selling papers and circulating library volumes these Secretaries carried pledge papers and so aided recruitment. Each quarter they delivered a report on their district to the Committee and were rewarded with a tea and some 'innocent amusement'. WBH believed that the 'efficient assistance' of these Secretaries was vital to the work of the committee.[79] Interestingly, one of the first youths entrusted with the responsibility of being a Superintendent was William John Harvey (no relation) who worked for many years on the *SWJ* before becoming co-owner in 1890. He was also a deacon of Zion Chapel and superintendent of the Frome BOH.[80]

By November 1863, WBH was able to report that membership of the Frome BOH stood at 2,205 (about 20% of Frome's population), 1709 being juveniles and 466 being adults. The BOH had held thirty-four meetings including monthly prayer meetings on a Sunday.[81] Earlier that year, WBH was invited to speak at the Eighth Annual Meeting of the United Kingdom Band of Hope Union, which was held at Exeter Hall in London. Other speakers included leading abstentionists Revs Burns and McCree so it seems that the Frome BOH was recognised nationally for its organisation. In this speech WBH stressed his belief in the importance of 'every amusement of an innocent character' and in particular 'the power of music… to refine and instruct the infant mind' but insisted on the even greater importance of 'sound instruction' so that children left each meeting not only happier but wiser Christians.[82] He repeated this last point in an article of 1880, wherein he stressed again the important work that older teenagers can do, even if they feel they have outgrown the meetings. As before, this work was mainly to do with monitoring the younger students but, by this time also included membership of the Frome Temperance Choral Union. WBH also asserted that a leader must 'be a good disciplinarian who would insist, in a kindly way, on perfect order'. He must also 'preside at all the meetings, arrange the programmes and take a general direction of proceedings'. This included rehearsing the recitations and 'securing the best speaker within his reach'.[83] This represents an enormous amount of work, so it is not surprising that he delegated the junior BOH Superintendent role to William John Harvey by 1882.

A bazaar held by Zion Congregational Church in the grounds of North Hill House c 1895. William Brett Harvey is seated in the centre wearing a bowler hat.

WBH was still Superintendent of Zion Sunday School and a Deacon at Zion Chapel at this stage, as well as secretary of the Frome BOH. It is also clear from Fred Knee's* Diary that WBH would give up his evenings for discussion and prayer meetings with the older boys. These were held at his house.[84]

Peter Clark, Who was Fred Knee? FSLS Yearbook 18, 2015. Ed

Probably the 1860s were the peak of Frome's influence at a national level, but it remained prominent at a regional level into the 20th century. In 1902, WBH gave two papers on 'aggressive temperance' in which he urged that temperance be taught at every Sunday School and that every church should have a connection with a Band of Hope. Temperance and Christianity should work hand in hand since 'the direct or indirect cause of the neglect of religious observance was drink'. Sport should be encouraged as a healthy entertainment, but church sports clubs should not permit alcohol or allow members to enter a public house in connection with any church activity. He also urged the provision of temperance refreshment rooms in every village and a campaign to remove alcohol from public meetings through the exercise of personal influence and public pressure. Music halls should be stopped from selling alcohol and vigilance committees should be formed to ensure that police and magistrates enforced the law. Finally they should ensure the election of right-minded people to public bodies and support all legislation that lessened the influence of the drink trade and they should be prepared to work with non-abstainers to achieve their goals. Thus would their use of all possible influence 'purify the amusements of the people' and England would become to a degree never yet attained 'a praise in the earth'.[85]

However serious the intent, the English temperance movement never lost sight of the need for people to enjoy themselves. At Frome, meetings of the BOH were of two sorts: public and members only, and the members meetings were generally intended to be of an 'entertaining character, either scientific experiments, dissolving views or music'. Speaking to the first Band of Hope Conference in Bristol in 1857, WBH was very clear that this was felt to be the best way to 'secure and maintain the interest of children...[86] We think it well to do all we can to gain the hearts of the children and make them love the Band of Hope; then what we say comes with more power than it would otherwise'.[87] The total number of meetings held, of all sorts, including village meetings, peaked in 1890 at an impressive 175.[88]

Important though routine was, the temperance movement knew that it needed specials and even spectaculars to grab people's attention. For example, early temperance fetes, held in fields on the outskirts of Frome, provided entertainment on a scale never before seen in that part of Somerset. Events always opened with a procession through town, many carrying flags or banners with mottoes such as *If sinners entice thee, consent thou not, Wine is a Mocker, Water is Best* and *Train up a child in the way he should go*. Mixed in with the marchers, who came from far and wide were several bands. One such procession reportedly took twenty minutes to pass a given point. In the fields were swings, roundabouts, donkey rides, target shooting stalls and so on.

Tents held working models, displays of the latest industrial processes and exotic items. There were organised games, food stalls, lectures, prize-givings and concerts. As darkness fell there were often fireworks, WBH himself setting them off. In later years these fetes became temperance picnics in the grounds of supportive gentry, such as Lord Cork at Marston and lost some of their drama, but always they demonstrated that thousands of people could get together and have an orderly yet fun time, and all without alcohol.[89]

More regularly, Frome's quarterly agricultural fair had with it an evening pleasure fair. The *SWJ* frequently deprecated the usual 'vice and wanton folly' of this 'motley group of cheap exhibitions,' and 'debasing attractions'.[90] Frome's weekly market was held in its central streets, hence the *SWJ*'s praise for all who strove to shield 'our industrial classes from the destructive allurements of the public-house',[91] hence also the regular counter-attractive 'shields,' many of which followed a similar pattern. There would be a late afternoon tea, followed by an evening entertainment. The entertainment would have a speech but would consist largely of teetotal and respectable songs. Prices and timings varied but, the adult charge for the entertainment, between 4d and 6d, was only the public-house's price of a couple of pints of beer. Many programmes, including all the songs, were advertised in advance in the *SWJ*.[92] These meetings were originally a BOH idea, but some of Frome's chapels soon organised parallel events.[93] By 1860, 'special efforts' were being made to offer wholesome counter-attractions at 'Christmas, Easter, Whitsuntide, and the fairs, and on Saturday evenings'.[94] Indeed one cannot read the *SWJ* in the 1860s and 1870s without discovering advertisements for and reports of a plethora of rational, respectable events, temperance entertainer Simeon Smithard being a frequent attraction.[95] As well as the events already described and the regular juvenile and adult temperance meetings, there were numerous lectures and readings, a choir and various night schools, excursions and sporting events.[96] For quieter times there was a reading room and coffee room and later a British Workman public-house (that is a public-house without alcohol).[97] An industrious worker would hardly have time to dig his potatoes.[98]

Very few of these activities were free, but their target was not the absolute poor but those working people whose limited discretionary spending could be directed. Rational recreation, as it was called, was intended to occupy the workers in acceptable 'regulated amusements', keep them in church, and away from 'drunkenness...brawling and ...fornication'.[99] At times the *SWJ* seemed out of touch with its readers, failing to understand why 'so many of the respectable portion of them sought amusement at a common circus while only 40 or 50 attended so engrossing and instructive address' on Japan.[100] Similarly, in attitude, it extolled the 'beneficial' alternative of madrigal concerts to the 'generally coarse and vicious' working men's entertainments in 1856.[101] However, WBH's focus on music was astute, since experiencing such activities often engenders the same sense of involvement and belonging that can be found in the public house. Humans can lose themselves in music as effectively as they can in alcohol, or, modern research shows, sex.[102] By the 1870s, even the anti-teetotalist *FT* saw these BOH counter-attractions as 'pleasing evenings' and as 'the means to prevent much evil'.[103]

Abbreviations:	WBH	William Brett Harvey
	BOH	Band of Hope
	FT	*Frome Times*
	SHC	Somerset Heritage Centre
	SWJ	*Somerset* and *Wilts Journal*
	WTH	*Bristol (*later *Western) Temperance Herald*

References are all available via info@fsls.org.uk

Part II of 'William Brett Harvey – A Busy Man' will follow. Ed

The Life of Betty Trask (1893–1983): Fiction, Fame, and Frome
by Peter Merchant

Nick Channer's book *Writers' Houses* [1] is a recent reminder of how indivisible our interest in an author's work normally is from an interest in his or her whereabouts. There is normally little difference, and no interval, between the marks that authors leave on literary history and the marks they make on local history. With the novelist Betty Trask, however, the alignment of the two is rather unusual. She never really made a name for herself with her books, and yet she put Frome on the map by having lived there.

The Register of 1939, taken in the early months of the war, only partly discloses her direction of travel. It notes that the occupation of Miss Margaret Elizabeth Lisle Trask, born 2 January 1893, is authoress; but the address is 54 Evelyn Gardens in Kensington, and for the Somerset connections it is her parents that need probing. The father, William, retired from his work in finance, banking and insurance, was born near Ilminster in July 1859 and turns out to have played nearly fifty games of county cricket for Somerset in the 1880s and 1890s, with a batting average of 14.41 and a bowling average of 37.83. The mother, still occupied in 1939 with unpaid domestic duties, was also called Margaret. She came from a Frome family: the Le Gros of North Hill House, who co-owned the Merchants Barton silk mill, now the Silk Mill Studios and Gallery. Initially, therefore, Betty Trask visited Frome in order to stay at North Hill House with her mother's relatives. The last of them, her aunt, lived until 1955.

North Hill House in 2020

Although North Hill House was then lost to her, Trask herself remained in Frome, living at 84 Oakfield Road. She put novel-writing behind her after 1957, by which time she had more than thirty books to her name, and lived out the last twenty-five years of her life very quietly. That her occupation had ever been Authoress was forgotten until, after her death on 25 January 1983, a bequest of around £400,000 to the Society of Authors was announced. The money went to fund a prize for first novels written by authors under the age of 35 'in a traditional or romantic, but not experimental, style.'

Début: novels of the 1920s

Now, with the books on whose spines and covers it used to be seen no longer in circulation, the Betty Trask Prize and Awards are all that make Trask's name familiar, if anything does. Although she may be known as a perennial handmaiden to the emergence of fresh literary talent, it is not generally realised that Trask herself, as a new author for Hodder and Stoughton, once joined in the fray. Her own emergence took place over the summer and autumn of 1928. In June, *The Ladies' Home Journal* published her story 'No String—to His Bow,' in an issue also featuring such well-established authors as John Galsworthy, Hugh Walpole, and (already) A A Milne. Then, at the end of September, Trask's first novel *Cotton Glove Country* was published by Hodder and Stoughton.

Betty Trask in 1928 shortly after the publication of Cotton Glove Country
Photo: The Tatler No 1428 7 Nov 1928

If the Betty Trask Prize and Awards had existed in 1928, *Cotton Glove Country* would not have won top honours; it would have had to compete with Evelyn Waugh's *Decline and Fall*. However, it won plaudits far and wide. 'Miss Trask has woven a delicate fairy-like story,' declared *The Brisbane Courier* on 12 January 1929. By 'delicate' it, of course, meant the opposite of action-packed. This very un-Waughlike novel has a heroine called Elizabeth who is twenty-six years old but still capable of saying 'nothing has ever happened to me, and I have never been anything else but a child. Away from her home in South Kensington, all that she has known is Mend, the 'mild provincial town' in Somerset in which her 'maiden aunt and bachelor uncle' live. As the August Bank Holiday approaches, Elizabeth takes the train from Paddington for a month's stay with Aunt Fay and Uncle Simon.

Trask's *Cotton Glove Country* shares a border with two works published in 1855. If the framework takes a hint from Ivan Turgenev's play *A Month in the Country*, the plot recalls Elizabeth Gaskell's novel *North and South*. *North and South*, a book by an Elizabeth about a Margaret, had its young heroine travelling far from home to a factory town whose cotton mills and Dissenting congregations feel alien to her, yet finding love there. *Cotton Glove Country*, a book by a

Margaret Elizabeth which gives the heroine the second of those names rather than the first, affords the same fulfilment to its central character in the form of romance with Quentin (Quin) Hilliard. He is the stranger with whom Elizabeth exchanged a few pleasantries on the train and whose stay in Mend happily coincides with hers. Even as they separately travelled out, there was magic in the air: 'Paddington Station was full of smoke. / It came like an enchantment, encircling the necks of a platform-full of excursionists in an embrace…'. When they return to London together as an engaged couple, the magic is still more palpable: 'Paddington Station was full of smoke. It came down like an enchantment, encircling Quentin and Elizabeth in bridal wreathes'.

Quentin apart, the novel is demonstrably autobiographical. For her first novel, Trask supplies a heroine created in her own image. Her name is Elizabeth, she is a resident of Kensington, and she is given the opportunity to travel west to Frome because her aunt and uncle have inherited a large house there that used to belong to her grandfather. Trask establishes the novel's principal setting as follows:

> Mend is built on two sharp little hills…
> Mend is full of chapels and factories. Elizabeth's grandfather, who established his family in the town, had been a pillar to one of the former and a pioneer in one of the latter. He died wealthily and in a manner befitting a pillar, leaving his family in a large house on top of one of the hills of Mend.

Elizabeth's grandfather is immediately recognisable as Trask's grandfather, Philip Edgar Le Gros; and North Hill House is the 'large house' which the novel will call Stillwood.

Another passenger on the train that Elizabeth and Quin both happen to have taken is a Somerset woman with 'hard-worked knuckles shining redly through thin cotton gloves darned at the finger-tips'. These cotton gloves are the insignia of provincial life, and mark Mend out as different from the kid-gloved Kensington. Trask's emphasis on the provinciality of a town whose name appeared to put it on the edge of the Mendips did not go down well in Frome. One trenchant passage on the local liking for door sausage draught excluders: 'red baize bags like boa-constrictors, stuffed with saw-dust', suggested a backwater borough intent on stopping its ears against the noise of the world, keeping the winds of change out, and keeping its mind closed. The folk of Frome never quite forgave Trask for the picture of the town that *Cotton Glove Country* had painted. They could not show her the same amused tolerance with which, on the other side of the Mendips and just a few years earlier, the people of Burnham-on-Sea had met Ben Travers when he held up the mirror to their town in *Rookery Nook*.

Trask's next novel, *Flute, Far and Near* (1929), is notably faithful to the template laid down in *Cotton Glove Country*. It has a nineteen-year-old heroine, the Flute of the title, and is structured around a Christmas and New Year holiday that she spends in 'the gentle, unassuming town of Withy'.

The town of Withy is built on two of the green hills of Somerset, by its presence turning both of them from green to grey. It is one of those happy, small Somersetshire towns, set in a land, green as a dear memory, under a modestly veiled sky.

The town of Withy has many endearing characteristics, such as roads too narrow to turn a cart in, and memorial fountains to worthy citizens, all well set up in the way of modern traffic.

It has certain visitable monuments, a confusion of Urban and Rural District Councils, plenty of the Poor that are always with us, and an undisturbed, brooding air.

In short, to visit the Town of Withy, you would say that here, at least, Time could not wreak much harm.

Should you climb its northerly grey hills and brave Granny's gates, drive, great trees, front door, a different complexion, decided as a hot blush, would be put upon your opinion.

Having grown up in Kensington, Flute is 'a town-child, born and bred'; but at Granny's hilltop home, Willow Hall, enchantment hangs heavy in the semi-rural air.

On this occasion there is a trauma that the magic will need to dispel. Flute has been shaken by a 'queer, unbelievable, Terrible Thing'. It emerges that she was a teenage bride who on the same day became a teenage widow. Her husband, Edward Whayman, was killed as the wedding party left the church. Then it emerges not only that 'Granny had been a widow herself ever since Flute's mother's girlhood' but that she is the Bessie whom we met on the eve of her marriage in the book's Prelude. The parallels between the grandmother's behaviour then and the granddaughter's behaviour now, vigorously spinning a globe to enjoy the rattling sound that it makes, lend a satisfying circularity to the story and reassure the reader that early widowhood does not necessarily throw the world off its axis. Finally, to complete Flute's recovery, Robin Simmons walks back into her life. He is this novel's equivalent of Quentin Hilliard: the stranger whom each heroine must have met before arriving at her destination and must then meet again in Somerset. The memory of the first meeting is even more radiant than it was in *Cotton Glove Country* because here the pair met not on the train but in a London toy-shop, where Robin helped Flute to buy the calico clown doll that supplies her with emotional support: 'Cob, that obliging spar'. In Withy, Flute kisses Robin on her twentieth birthday, and all else seems to recede into the distance:

How far everything was!
Nothing near but the feel of silken strands over her own heart.

This is the exact mid-point of the novel, and it is in these words that its title is explained.

That love comes looking for Flute in Withy, as it did for Elizabeth in Mend, is part of the rite of passage which both books emphasise. Each of the first two heroines is a young woman on the cusp of maturity who goes west and finds that the Somerset surroundings consolidate her growth:

Flute had, in fact, made friends with no one except Nurse, her fairy-story books and her own fancies. A pretty enough arrangement, while Flute, a child, need only hang the tree of Life with tinsel and toys. But when that tree was ready to be planted out in the world...!

There is no reason to assume that Trask's own experience of growing out of girlhood corresponded precisely to Elizabeth's or Flute's, but the scenes and locations, Kensington and Somerset, are the same. Flute even 'possessed a birthday just in the New Year', which, as well as ensuring that her stay in Withy at the turning of the year, is palpably a farewell to her teenage self, with the old rung out and the new rung in, means that she probably shares Trask's birthday, 2 January.

Trask had good warrant for giving her first two works of fiction an autobiographical basis. She was replicating some of the strategies which, as used over the previous ten years by Virginia Woolf, had made Woolf's one of the most powerful and original voices in the literature of the 1920s. Virginia Woolf grew up in Hyde Park Gate in South Kensington, within a mile of Evelyn Gardens. The summers of her girlhood were spent in a hilltop property, Talland House, just outside St Ives in Cornwall. Her 1927 novel *To the Lighthouse*, published a year before Trask's début, alchemised Woolf's memories of Cornwall, and it is in that process, 'the transforming of personal memory into impersonal art, that her biographer Lyndall Gordon locates 'the obsessive drama of Virginia Woolf'[2].

Woolf wanted this admission into fiction of personal memories to strike a blow against the kind of Edwardian writing that she deplored: writing which took an altogether unexceptional life and rendered it in all its material detail. Arnold Bennett might look to 'the average young man who arrives at Waterloo at 9.40 every morning'[3], but Woolf aimed at something much more subjective and impalpable. The impressions of the individual were of far greater interest to her than information about the type. In her novel *Night and Day* (1919) Woolf exposes the 'flotsam and jetsam' of Mary Datchet's thinking by opening Mary's mind to us at a time when her thoughts begin to drift this way and that, with the business from which they branch off lying sunken underneath. The 'little fragmentary phrases' with which the canvas of the heroine's consciousness is in this way splashed are increasingly used by Woolf to carry the main weight of the story. She accordingly abandons the 'formal railway line of sentence' which in a letter to Jacques Raverat (3 October 1924) she says she associates with Arnold Bennett, and seeks to write an altogether more fluid and flexible style. Trask's concern to follow the flux and reflux of Flute's thinking pushes her into similar stylistic experimentation in *Flute, Far and Near*:

Flute lay in bed for three days staring at her bedroom ceiling.
Then she got up, feeling as though she had received a severe shaking the last thing last night.
The house looked quite different when she went downstairs into it.

From what seems different in the house, Trask then turns inward, to what is different now in Flute:

> The shaking had, somehow, emptied her heart. If it's really your heart you feel with, Flute's felt as empty as a child's money-box on Christmas Eve. Nothing at all left in it.
> Gently, Flute held her heart to her ear, as it were, and shook it. Not even a dry leaf fluttered inside it.... Wasn't Flute shocked? Sad? Nothing suitable?... Not even plain sorry? Flute shook her heart afresh ... no answer rattled inside it....

The clipped and elliptical prose sits strangely against Trask's subsequently expressed preference for solidly traditional writing but is perfect for conveying Flute's numbed state of mind as the Terrible Thing sends ripple after ripple up to the surface.

Finale: novels of the 1950s

The two books by which Trask's achievement at the latter end of her career can most conveniently be gauged, since Somerset Libraries currently hold two copies of each, are *And Confidential* (1953) and the final work, *The Merry Belles of Bath* (1957). These are also the only two of Trask's novels to have been posthumously reprinted, both in 1984, although *And Confidential* is not typical of her overall output. The book begins with an estate agent arriving at a country mansion to value its contents, but then turns into Trask's nearest approach to Daphne du Maurier and Alfred Hitchcock. As if she were rearranging some of the elements of *Rebecca*, Trask introduces secrets that we must wait to see unlocked, thickens the plot with the involvement of an unseen Miss Danvers, and even has a house burning down.

Although *The Merry Belles of Bath* uses South Kensington as a secondary setting, it is true to its title in laying the scene mainly in Bath. Jane Austen is an obvious model both for the way the novel registers Bath's social whirl and for its marriage plot. Five daughters, whose surname is not Bennet but Burn-Belton, enter the matrimonial stakes and prove themselves 'natural huntresses'. The date of the action is the end of Victoria's reign, a hundred years after Austen, which enables Trask to draw on her childhood memories. Even the team mates that Trask's father had had in his county career: 'the great cricketer, Sammy Woods himself', and 'dear, delightful, sporty Arthur Newton', fleetingly appear. As the names of both people and places slide into the text, they are all lifted out of real life into the heady atmosphere of romance. One of the five daughters dies suddenly of thrombosis, three chapters from the end, but still the romance survives. The 'silken strands' that Trask liked to wind around all that she wrote have a surprising tensile strength.

Afterlife

In early 1983, within seven weeks of each other, two ninety-year-old women writers passed away. The first, on 25 January, was Betty Trask. The second was Dame Rebecca West, who died in Kensington on 15 March. She had been born, as Cecily Isabel Fairfield, just twelve days before Trask. The two lives were thus almost exactly coextensive; but the public profiles could hardly have been more different. Betty Trask no longer had one. Rebecca West not only had to her name one of the most celebrated novels to have come out of the First World War, *The Return of the Soldier* (1918), but was famed besides for her long affair with H G Wells, which produced a son, and for her political activism. She had named herself after an Ibsen heroine, and had been both a socialist and a suffragette. Betty Trask, neither a famously free spirit in her youth nor a grand dame in her retirement, appeared by comparison to have led the circumscribed life of an old maid.

Yet Trask was about to claim attention worldwide. Like Miss Danvers in *And Confidential*, she left a will that was bound to raise eyebrows. The size of the bequest to the Society of Authors attracted attention; and in some quarters the conditions attached to it, stipulating that only works of a traditional nature would be considered for awards, drew mockery. Posthumously, therefore, Trask was in the public eye. Yet what had put her there was not a renewed interest in the books themselves but a sudden curiosity about the woman behind them. Since any of Trask's own novels were reissued, in fact, there has, to date, already been time for a hundred living novelists to draw four-figure sums from the fund that her bequest set up, and it would not be surprising if before the next reissue that roll of honour contained the names of a hundred more.

Curiosity about Betty Trask reached its peak four months after her death, with an extraordinary essay for the magazine *Caretas* by the Peruvian writer and subsequent Nobel Laureate, Mario Vargas Llosa. Vargas Llosa's essay, which as 'La señorita de Somerset': 'The Spinster of Somerset', was later gathered into the third volume of his selected writings[4], is a misleading but magnificent piece of myth-making. The parts which are plausible seem propped up by some wildly wishful surmises. Vargas Llosa is convincing about the circumstances in which Trask came to settle in Frome, after the death of her father in 1949, and the shape of her time in the town: thirty years in her own small and unshowy house, 'su modesta casita de Oakfield Road,' where to begin with she looked after her elderly mother, followed by five in a nursing home. His account of Trask's books, however, turns the delicate, fairy-like stories that the first reviewers saw into overheated bodice-rippers whose stock-in-trade consists:

> *de labios ardientes que al rozar los dedos marfileños de las jovencitas hacen que estas se abran al amor como las rosas y de cuchillos que se hunden con sangrienta ternura en el corazón de los amantes infieles.*

of ardent lips whose every touch on the ivory fingers of young women produces a rose-like efflorescence of passion, and of knives lovingly plunged into the hearts of unfaithful lovers.*

Mario Vargas Llosa

Vargas Llosa wants and needs to represent Trask's fiction as sensational because his principal point in the essay is that her books are utterly unlike her experience of the world:

Lo más extraordinario en la vida de Margaret Elizabeth Trask, que dedicó su existencia a leer y escribir sobre el amor, es que no tuvo en sus 88 años una sola experiencia amorosa.

The most extraordinary fact about the life of Margaret Elizabeth Trask, who dedicated her entire existence to reading and writing about love, is that through all her eighty-eight years she never once tasted it herself. *

Eighty-eight is of course a slight underestimate; and Vargas Llosa cannot know that his 'never once' is not underestimating Trask too. Ensuring complete accuracy is less important, however, than putting across the paradox that this author who wrote so lyrically, and even luridly, of love was herself a complete novice in the affairs of the heart and the least worldly of women:

Nunca hizo vida social, salió muy poco, profesó una amable alergia por los varones y jamás admitió un galanteo.

She never had any social life, scarcely ever ventured out, sheltered behind her apparent mild allergy to contact with males, and resisted all amorous advances.*

The more uneventful Vargas Llosa can show the life that Trask really lived to have been, the more evident it will become that all the fire and the vividness for which he thinks it is human to hunger had long since fled for her into the life of the imagination. When Trask took up her pen she constructed an imaginary world for which she was happy to abandon the real world as she knew it:

Dedicó sus días y sus noches a la fantasía y redujo lo que se llama vivir a lo mínimamente indispensable.

She dedicated her days and nights to the imagination and reduced the business of living, as we generally conceive of it, to an absolute minimum.*

The huge gap between fantasy and reality to which the essay consequently claims that the case of Betty Trask should alert the world is treated by Vargas Llosa as underlining the deep need in us all for literature and other forms of artistic creation. Through them we can enjoy an existence more glorious than we would ever otherwise know.

Vargas Llosa's position on Trask became plainer still when he joined in the celebrations marking the 400th anniversary of Cervantes's *Don Quixote*. The resulting essay was published in 2005.[5] It salutes Cervantes for taking as his subject a man whose books become a means of entry into a fantasy life that is rich literally beyond belief. What the novel therefore shows is that a dream such as will outshine our actual surroundings is art's precious gift to us all:

> *a través de la creación artística, el hombre puede romper los límites de su condición ... a través de la ficción los seres humanos logran romper los límites en que viven encarcelados ...*

> through artistic creation, humankind is able to break free from the limits of the human condition ... through stories we humans can contrive to transcend the imprisoning confines to which life accustoms us ...*

Trask is not mentioned by name in the essay on *Don Quixote*. However, by detailing the lessons that he takes this prototypical novel of world literature to have taught, Vargas Llosa's essay confirms that for him Betty Trask likewise embodies the essence of all that fiction is: proof positive of the power of the pipedream, the ability of the storyteller to fashion what is routine and run-of-the-mill into something illustrious and intense. Both Don Quixote as a reader of chivalric romances and Betty Trask as a writer of romantic fiction have managed to demonstrate that exercising the imagination can bring colour and excitement to the most humdrum provincial life, whether it is being lived out in La Mancha or in the Mendips.

Thus it is that Betty Trask, weaving her web of romance in defiance of the reality that surrounded her, becomes for Vargas Llosa an exemplary figure: not just the spinster of Somerset but Frome's very own Female Quixote. He slots her into a role by which she and her work are in some ways disparaged, yet in other ways mythically enlarged and resoundingly vindicated. Trask's novels may have seen the emphatic happy ending as fitter for dolls than for human beings, as when the closing words of *Flute, Far and Near* are given to Cob the Clown: 'a happy ending seems all right to me', but they still reached towards one whenever they could. Perhaps Mario Vargas Llosa's improbable mythologising of Trask has supplied a sort of happy ending for the novelist herself.

*Author's translations

[1] Channer N, *Writers' Houses,* Robert Hale, 2015
[2] Gordon L, *Virginia Woolf: A Writer's Life;* OUP, 1984
[3] Bennett A, *The Reasonable Life,* 1907
[4] Vargas Llosa M, *Contra viento y marea,* Seix Barral, Barcelona
[5] Vargas Llosa M, *Los cuatro siglos del Quijote,* Centro des Estudios Publicos, Santiago, Chile

Memories of Betty Trask
by Eunice Overend

I came back to Frome from the embryo Wildfowl Trust in 1949 when my mother had a stroke and, before returning to teaching, earned my keep by various part-time jobs. One of these was as gardener at North Hill House while the Head Gardener was ill, and I remember very well the Trask family staying with Miss Le Gros, as they had lost their London home in the bombing. There was no love lost between the two sisters. One would come out and talk to me as I weeded or pruned the shrubs, then, when she went in, the other, who had been peeping through the curtains, would appear, saying 'Don't you believe a word of what she's been telling you about me!' Miss Le Gros' resentment seemed to be because she considered that they had spent their share of the family money having a good time in London while she had carefully saved hers, and was now having to spend it giving them a home. They had the use of a small back sitting room next to the kitchen while the rest of the house was unused. The big room where later the Council met was a complete Victorian relic, full of valuable family bits and pieces, many of which Miss Le Gros told me she had left to the museum of the Literary and Scientific Institution so that they would be preserved in Frome.*

Mrs Trask was a lively old lady who could well stand up to her sister's shrewishness. Betty would sometimes talk through the open window, while her father, tall in his panama hat, wandered round the garden. His family had owned Ham Hill quarries, famous for the golden stone from which Montacute House and many mid-Somerset churches were built. I told them of sleeping up there when cycling from Exeter, watching fox cubs mouse jumping in the long grass at dusk, and, after dusk, a small air raid on Taunton. Betty wanted me to take her for a long drive at night, (I had an Austin Ruby by then), as she needed to describe it in something she was writing, but for some reason the plan fell through.

Before we lived here my mother and I used to spend summer holidays in Clift's Buildings with my grandmother. My uncle, Herbert Weaver[1], was churchwarden at St John's and I well remember the gossip and consternation when 'Cotton Glove Country' came out with Vicar Randolph and many local worthies but thinly-disguised and the rivalries between St John's and Zion there for all to see. I borrowed it from the library at that time and read it with a mixture of amusement at Frome remembered and sympathy for the very restricted life it was evident Betty must have led, though she had succeeded in plucking from it the background for her novel, but I have never been able to get hold of a copy since.

I often wondered, after Betty Trask moved to her terrace house in Oakfield Road, if she was alright, and if, as she grew old, she had enough money to live comfortably, but no one seemed to know. I guess I was right, though, in thinking that my brief gardening acquaintance would not have been considered sufficient excuse for a call just to find out.

* Sadly most of these were dispersed at auction in the late 1970s. Ed

This article by Eunice Overend first appeared in Contact January-June 1986 and was followed by a letter in Contact July-December 1986 from Mrs Phillippa Wilson of Ditcheat House

My sisters and I have just come to live in Somerset after many years, and I was most interested to see a copy of Contact, in which there was an article headed 'Betty Trask' by Eunice Overend, in which she mentioned doing garden work at North Hill during the war (sic). The article is so full of inaccuracies, that I feel that I must correct a few.

North Hill belonged to Miss Le Gros* who was our aunt, being the eldest sister of our father, Thomas Arthur Le Gros. She was a very gentle, kind, if somewhat strict person and we were devoted to her. We spent many months at North Hill at the time of, and after my Grandmother's death.

The Trasks (who, less said about the better) occupied the Smoking Room (the only room that had a gas fire) and was in the west wing, the kitchen being in the east wing. They also had a big double bedroom and dressing room, and another single bedroom, also the housekeeper's room where Betty was supposed to write. There was one fire in the house, being wartime, where my Aunt had to sit. The Trasks owned a house in Evelyn Gardens in London, which, as far as I know, was not bombed.

[1]*Catherine Hanley, FSLS Yearbook 15, 2012*

* Miss Le Gros died in 1955. Ed

FROME PETTY SESSIONS, *March 28.*—Messrs. John and Thomas Porter, clothiers, Frome, were summoned to answer the complaint of Samuel Savill Kent, sub-inspector of factories, charged with having employed Fanny Reynolds more than 10 hours, in a factory situate at Wallbridge, in their occupation, on the 13th March last, contrary to the statute in such case made and provided. The defendants admitted the offence charged, and were fined in the mitigated penalty of 20s., and 11s. costs.—Defendants were also charged with neglecting to hang up a notice in the said factory, pursuant to the Act. Defendants admitted the offence, and were fined £2, and 9s. 6d. cost. There were several other summonses against the defendants : they were withdrawn, on payment of costs.—*Daniel Trotman*, clothier, Frome, was summoned for the like offences, and amerced in the like fines.

My thanks to ALM for this article from the Devizes and Wilts Gazette, 4 April 1850. Samuel Savill Kent was the father of Savill Kent who was murdered at Rode Hill House in 1860. Ed

The Restoration of Emma Sheppard's Grave** at Trinity Church
(July-August 2019)
by Jim White

Emma Sheppard first came to my attention when reading Nick Hersey's story of her life[1]. The article enlightened me to Emma's remarkable active life devoted to women and children who were suffering straightened circumstances in early to mid-19th century Frome, during a transitional period from hand weaving and mill work to a machine-led manufacturing process. The lack of employment must have had a severe effect on local women and their children. With her strong Christian faith to guide her, Emma stepped into this difficult and contentious situation.

Alastair and Marie-Louise MacLeay discovered the monument under a yew tree and cleared away years of accumulated debris and undergrowth that covered the grave. The broken cross and shaft were found thrown down behind the block base stone.

A photograph of the grave by Cliff Howard[1] shows a cross lying on the ground with its broken shaft and base stone very discoloured. As a lifelong resident of Frome, I decided to offer my restoration skills to the Frome Society to restore what remained as a testament to Emma's work and dedication to those in desperate need.

On first examination, owing to their discolouration, I thought that the stones were from the Bath mines, but this soon proved to be wrong; they were white marble with inset lead block lettering in very good condition. The 510x610mm block base with ogee mould was set on a Forest of Dean base stone*, the whole sinking slightly to the North. Although very stained, the marble improved at once with cleaning but the deep staining was impossible to eradicate, however, the cross and shaft were not so straightforward; they were made by 'Mr Chapman of Portway, Frome using the most modern methods', and, although the base stone was faultless, its superstructure was a design disaster!

On taking the cross and shaft to my workshop to drill and dowel I was astounded by their weight: 25kg, the same as a bag of cement. The marble shaft, 100x130x460mm was quite inadequate to support this weight and I would expect it to have cracked into pieces after little more than 10 years. During restoration there was evidence to suggest that a repair had previously been undertaken.

When drilling the central section of the shaft from both ends to make a dowel repair, the marble split vertically, rendering it useless. On drilling the remains, still fixed to the base block, the same thing happened revealing a 15x100mm brass dowel fixed firmly in the stone. This left me only one alternative: to square the bottom of the cross and fix it on the short dowel with epoxy resin, which has now been completed and is secure.

The grave is bordered by an oblong ledge 1000x2150mm which once had a cast iron rail which has disappeared. I plan to clear the surface soil and lay washed limestone chippings to complete the restoration.

I would like to thank the Vicar of Trinity Church, Rev Graham Owen, and Alastair MacLeay for their help in the restoration of this important grave.

The grave after restoration

Forest of Dean stone was used widely by monumental masons and 'took a good letter.' Its use spread with the canal and rail systems of the 19th century, however, it suffers very badly with frost and rain in exposed positions which cause it to split

*

*For those who wish to visit Emma Sheppard's grave: enter the churchyard via the wicket gate, walk down the path and follow the first path to the left which leads to the West of the church. After 40m her grave is on the right. Ed

[1] Hersey N, FSLS Yearbook 20, 2017

The Frome Vinegar Brewery - A short history of the building from the mid-19th Century to the present Day

by John Corfield

When I joined Frome's Men's Shed, I was asked by the owner of the building, Sue Moloney, to investigate its history. This article is based on the research that I carried out which was based mainly on newspaper reports available on line, records at Frome Museum and the Somerset Heritage Centre.

The old 'Vinegar Works' in 2019

The old Vinegar Brewery has taken on various names such as 'Welsh Mill', 'Welshmill Vinegar Works,' the 'Welshmill Hub' etc and I was further confused by a drawing[1] in the V&A collections by Walter Spradbery. This was clearly a different building next to the river, so I compared the OS 1885 map[2] with that of today[3] and realised that the building had always been a 'Vinegar Works', but with the demolition of the mill, following alterations to the course the of river bed, the name Welsh Mill had been transferred to it.

Welsh Mill Frome c1940

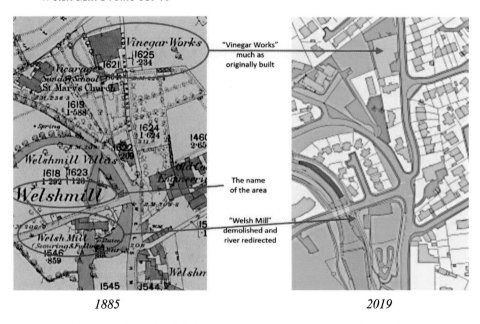

1885   2019

The 1840 tithe map shows Welsh Mill but no vinegar brewery, whereas both are present on the OS 1885 map; Lady Mary's Spring Lane runs past the building which is just south of the spring. The leasehold of the vinegar brewery was sold in 1905 as part of the Marston Estate sale from which it can be inferred that the building was completed in 1871. It is interesting to compare the outlines of the buildings and how little they have changed over 150 years.

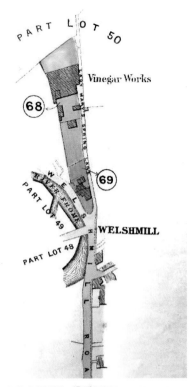

A number of well-secured FREEHOLD GROUND RENTS, situated in the Town of Frome and in the Village of Truddoxhill.

No. of Lot.	Description.	Date of Commencement of Lease.	Date of Termination of Lease.	No. of Years unexpired from Lady-day, 1905.	Ground Rent, per Annum.	Total Ground Rent.	Estimated Rack Rental.	Remarks.
					£ s. d.	£ s. d.	£ s. d.	
68	Vinegar Works and Garden adjoining, situated at Welsh Mill	25th Mar., 1871	25th Mar., 1966	61	11 0 0	11 0 0	60 0 0	
69	A Pair of Villas adjoining the above, and known as Mill View and Brookside	,, 1867	,, ,,	,,	6 0 0	6 0 0	30 0 0	

Marston Estate Sale& Vinegar Works Ground Rent

The earliest record of vinegar production comes from the *Isle of White Times*[4] of 19 October 1876 which indicates that the factory was run as a partnership of Richmond and Clarke, however, the partnership was dissolved the following year as reported in the *Salisbury and Winchester Journal* of 10 March 1877[5]. By 1883 James Richardson had taken on Percival Hodgson as partner as announced in the *Western Advertiser*[6] and they were later joined by Percival's father although this latter partnership was dissolved on 31 December 1887 as reported in the *London Gazette*[7] on 3 January 1888.

A CONSERVATIVE CANDIDATE.—After beating the bush for some time the Conservative party in Frome have hit upon a candidate in succession to Mr. L. H. Isaacs, who has retired. The gentleman selected is A. Hodgson, Esq., of Clopton-house, Stratford-on-Avon, a magistrate for the county of Warwick, and father of Mr. Percival S. Hodgson, who is in partnership with Mr James Richmond, of the Frome Vinegar Works. It is understood that Mr. A. Hodgson is exceedingly wealthy, having, it is said, amassed his fortune in Australia.

A New Partnership 1883

NOTICE is hereby given, that the Partnership heretofore subsisting between us the undersigned, James Richmond, Perceval Septimus Hodgson, and Sir Arthur Hodgson, K.C.M.G., carrying on business as Vinegar Manufacturers at Frome, in the county of Somerset, under the style or firm of Richmond and Company, has been dissolved, by mutual consent, as and from the 31st day of December, 1887.—Dated the 31st day of December, 1887.

James Richmond.
Arthur Hodgson.
Perceval S. Hodgson.

The Partnership dissolved 1887

VINEGAR BREWERY AT FROME SOMERSET.
MESSRS.
ALFRED THOMAS, PEYER, AND MILES Will SELL BY AUCTION, at THE MART, LONDON, on MONDAY, 26th March, at One o'clock (unless previously disposed of by Private Contract),—

THE FROME VINEGAR WORKS, for some years carried on by Messrs. Richmond and Co., and held upon lease for a long term at a nominal ground rent.
The Premises occupy a large site, and are well supplied with water. They consist of the Brewery, fitted with a 25qr. plant, and which, with the Goodwill of the existing Trade (the foundation of a largely-extended future connection), will be included in the Sale.
The situation is within easy access of Bristol and other large towns in the West of England and South Wales, and thus well placed for extending the trade.
A portion of the purchase can be left on mortgage.
Particulars may be had of Messrs. Cruttwell, Daniel, and Cruttwells, Solicitors, Frome; of Messrs. Tansley-Witt and Edgell, Accountants, 40 Chancery Lane, W.C.; and of Messrs. Alfred Thomas, Peyer, and Miles, Brewery Auctioneers and Valuers, 2 Adelaide Place, London Bridge, E.C.

There must have been problems, since the factory was put up for auction as advertised in the *Gloucestershire Chronicle*[8] of 24 March 1888.

However, it was again up for auction as reported in the *Gloucester Chronicle* of 1 October 1890.[9]

It has not been possible to follow the ownership from this date until after World War II although there are references to Frome Vinegar Brewery Co, but not how the Company was incorporated.

Notice of Auction in March 1888

86

THE FROME VINEGAR WORKS, FROME, SOMERSET.

MESSRS.
ALFRED THOMAS, PEYER, & MILES

Will SELL BY AUCTION, on WEDNESDAY, 29th Oct., THE FROME VINEGAR WORKS, occupying a large site, and well supplied with water. They consist of the Brewery, fitted with a 25-quarter Mash Tun and all necessary Utensils. The Property is held upon lease for a long term at a nominal ground rent, and being within easy access of Bristol and other populous towns in the West of England and South Wales the situation is a favourable one, and stands exceedingly well for developing the business in those districts.

Particulars may be had of Messrs. Alfred Thomas, Peyer, and Miles, Brewery Auctioneers and Valuers, 2 Adelaide Place, London Bridge, London, E.C.

Notice of Auction in October 1890

Meanwhile, the vinegar factory had been operating as shown by the advertisement to sell 'grain wash suitable for pigs' which appeared in the *Frome Times*[10] from November 1881 until March 1882.

FOR SALE, a quantity of GRAIN WASH, suitable for Pigs.—Apply at the VINEGAR WORKS, Frome.
[2782]

Another report in the *Frome Times*[10] about the 'Polluted state of the River Frome' involved the Vinegar Works: *On 30th May last Mr GR Wilson of Welshmill made complaint of a nuisance from a pond in Mr Bulman's garden. This was found to arise from offensive matter sent into the pond from some Vinegar works a short distance off, but outside the borough. Being thus beyond the limits of the Board's jurisdiction, the matter was referred to the Rural Sanitary Authority and the nuisance was abated.* Vinegar production continued since there was an advertisement for a salesman in the *Western Daily Press*[11] on 27 November 1890.

WANTED, a TRAVELLER, having a good connection, and calling upon Grocers in the West of England and South Wales, to Represent the Frome Vinegar Brewery Co., Frome. —Apply by letter.

Advertisement for Salesman

The *Western Chronicle*[12] of 21 September 1894 reported a fatal accident at Writhlington.

87

RADSTOCK.

A SERIOUS ACCIDENT occurred on Saturday evening to a carter named Hamlett, in the employ of the Frome Vinegar Works. Hamlett had been to Radstock with a load of vinegar, and had returned to the Countess Waldegrave's Frome Hill Depot, and loaded the vehicle with coal. He left the depôt all right, but had only gone a little way on the road when he slipped from the waggon, and both wheels passed over his body, inflicting terrible internal injuries. Sergt. Sharpe had him removed to the Fir Tree Inn, where he was attended to by Dr. Worger.

The report of a fatal accident

The Fir Tree Inn

Two advertisements in the *Bath Chronicle* in 1918 showed that the brewery continued to prosper, the first on 23 March[13] was for an 'ineligible [sic] STRONG MAN', which may not have been successful, since the second on 2 November[14] requested 'Willing MARRIED MEN' with 'good references'.

STRONG MAN wanted at once; ineligible. Permanent.—Vinegar Brewery Frome

TWO or three Strong, Willing MARRIED MEN wanted for Brewery Work in Frome. Good wages. Must live in the town, and have good references. Permanency if satisfaction given.— The Vinegar Brewery Frome

Advertisements for Workers

Apart from a small addition to the main building which is shown on the OS 1930 map, there are no changes to the premises until the 1950s and the road next to the plant remained 'Lady Mary's Spring Lane'.

The Vinegar Brewery was acquired by British Vinegars Ltd of Bristol soon after the end of World War II, probably 1946, since the *Somerset Standard* of 23 February and 10 June 1951 report on the enquiry into the refusal of planning permission to extend the factory buildings. The British Vinegar factory had suffered war damage and had not been permitted to reinstate their building in Bristol, hence they wished to transfer all operations to Frome, where vinegar brewing was taking place. British Vinegars acquired land next to the factory to extend it, however, planning permission was refused in February 1951 since this land was scheduled for residential development, being close to the centre of the town. British Vinegar's appeal was dismissed in June 1951, so all operations could not be transferred, which led to the end of vinegar brewing in Frome, although the date of closure is not known.

By 1959, the building had been taken over by Benchairs. From 1959 to 1971, there are a series of planning applications by Benchairs, who were assembling and storing chairs and other furniture from Eastern Europe in the building. There was a massive fire in September

1970 which had started in the warehouse, lasted for 48 hours and caused serious damage. In 1978, the building was bought by the family business of Ray and Mary Wadey, Micro Precision Instruments, manufacturers of medical and electronic equipment. During the coming 30 years, there are a series of planning applications showing that the building was in multiple occupation; this has led to objections from local residents on account of various business uses. For instance, in 1984, there were seven subunits in the building, being used for newspaper distribution, precision engineering, metalwork, the repair and sale of pianos, making harpsichords and invalid chair controls. At other times, it has been used for offices, laser cutting, upholstery, photography studios and education.

Sue Moloney, who has managed the building since 2012, is currently considering the sale to Edventure, a cooperative, which would continue to run it as a diverse business community, bring the building into community ownership and use it as a local hub.

Acknowledgements:

Thanks to Brian Marshall of Frome Museum for patiently searching the archives and to Alastair MacLeay and Mick Davis for documents relating to the sale of the Vinegar Works in 1905 and 1951 respectively.

References are available through info@fsls.org.uk

On Monday, at St. Peter's church, Frome, by the Rev. J. B. Clarke, Wm. Toop, aged 89, to Mary Barrow, aged 52, being his fourth wife! Toop has recently declared that he would prefer a younger woman, but he was fearful of having a young family. Prior to his marriage he went to a jeweller's shop for a wedding ring, which was instantly handed to him as a present. After the nuptial knot was tied, they were regaled at the house of an honest baker, near the church, with refreshment, and while partaking of the same, a party appeared in the front of the house with a drum, fife, and other music, and after playing for some time, the bride and bridegroom, with the band, proceeded to the Pack Horse Inn, accompanied by a concourse of followers. After partaking of a cup or two of ale, the bridegroom danced a hornpipe, and requested his wife, in the most loving terms, to join him, which she refused on account of her never having learnt to dance. They then retired to their home to enjoy themselves as they pleased. Toop, for the last 50 years has been well known in Frome and the neighbourhood, as a vendor of vegetables and water-cresses; in crying the latter, which was generally in the evening, his voice being very shrill, he has often been heard at the distance of two miles. Toop resided for nearly fifty years at Corsly, Wilts, which is a distance from Frome of about four miles, and he went nearly two miles farther to obtain his cresses, and was regular in Frome with them every day, Sundays excepted, parading the town for several hours. It is consequently supposed that during the last 50 years he has travelled 100,000 miles. Toop never would strike either of his wives, for he considered it unmanly, but did not hesitate to drag them backward and forward over a large gooseberry bush, which was in the front of his house, if they transgressed!

I am grateful to ALM for this cutting from the Bristol Mirror, 20 October 1832. Ed

The Cockey Lamps and Cockeys of Frome
by Mary Canale, Sue Latham and Ric Swann

Cockey street lamps are unique and can be seen all around Frome. The local historian Prebendary Daniel, stated that Lewis Cockey came from Warminster to Frome about 1680 and set up a bell foundry at 45 Milk Street and later in Bell Lane in what would become the Trinity Area. Church bells cast by the Cockeys from the mid-17th to the mid-19th century were of good quality and were installed all over the West Country. The Cockey descendants took a prominent part in the church and public life of Frome; another Lewis Cockey, a brazier, was granted a lease of 15 Bath Street in 1773, which finally expired in 1859. Meanwhile Christopher Cockey had been granted a lease on 24 Bath Street by the Earl of Cork in 1786 and his eldest son, Edward had built a new house on the site by 1823. In 1822 Edward was listed as a 'Boot & Shoemaker' as well as 'Iron Monger and Iron & Brass Founder' in Bath Street, Frome. He had decided that bell casting was no longer a paying proposition, seeing the gas industry expanding, he changed from casting bells to gas components and general engineering. He was joined by two of his brothers, Henry and Francis Cockey, both able engineers and by 1861 the firm was employing 125 men and 41 boys.

The Frome Gas Company was set up in 1831 with Edward Cockey as Secretary and the first house to have gas lighting was 7 Bath Street that November. The foundry had been casting street furniture: bollards, railings, gate posts and drain covers and when gas was introduced to the town, the company designed, manufactured and erected the first street gas lamps. These continued to be used until the introduction of electricity in 1903. The foundry was behind the cottages in Rook Lane and Palmer Street; when it became too small, it was transferred to a new site

Cockey Gate post at Egford

90

A corner of the Market Place showing one of the original gas lamps c1865

in Garston, built in 1893 which covered four and a half acres with its own rail sidings off the Radstock line in Wallbridge. In 1886 Cockeys had become a limited company.

The new works at Garston designed, manufactured and erected gas works in all parts of the globe but particularly in South Wales and the West of England. Their main business was the design and manufacture of gas holders, standards, boilers and iron roofs. The Cockey Company took out several patents on various designs, the most important being the Patent Washer Scrubber which completely recovered tar as well as ammonia, carbon dioxide and hydrogen sulphide from coal gas.

During World War I Cockeys were a Controlled Establishment and manufactured an immense quantity of materials with such satisfaction that the firm received a special letter of appreciation and thanks from the Admiralty. They were also on the lists of the War Office and the Crown Agents and had an office in Victoria Street, London.

The company ceased trading in 1960 and there is now only one male Cockey left in Britain, however, in 1634 Thomas Cockey travelled on the *Bonaventure* to America. He eventually arrived in Maryland, where, being a gentleman, he was granted some land and today there are about 350 members of the Cockey family living in Cockeysville, Maryland, north of Baltimore, including a Judge, Joshua F Cockey, so the name will continue, just not in England.

After three years of meetings featuring The Electric Lighting Scheme for Frome, the Frome Urban District Council held a special

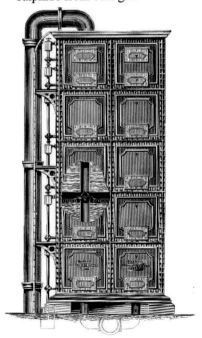

The Cockey Patent Washer Scrubber

meeting in February 1904 at the Public Offices to discuss the selection of the replacement tops of the Cockey lamps from gas to electricity. There were two patterns selected, one was cast iron and the other wrought iron. Manager Mr Nicholl of Edmondson's Electric Corporation, the company chosen to carry out the changes from gas to electricity, said: *the standards were not only submitted for their [Councillors] approval, but also that they might see the difference between an inferior and an excellent one. The superior bracket designed and made by Messrs Singers' Works, was the finest he had seen for a considerable time and as far as his experience went, he did not think they could better it.* Although the wrought iron bracket was more expensive than the cast iron one, the council members were in favour of keeping the business within the town and the Singers' Art Metal Works design for the 80 candle power incandescent lamps was approved.

It was reported in the *Somerset Standard* in May 1904 that: *The installation of the works was commenced on 3 November last, when the first length of cable was laid in Portway and since then, in spite of the unprecedented wet weather experienced during the winter and early spring, very satisfactory progress has been made. Between 10 and 11 miles of cable has been laid and on Monday the standards for street lighting were delivered and the erection of the arc and other lamps speedily carried out, as well as the conversion of the gas lamps. It is hoped that this work will be completed by early next month. In all there are to be 10 arc lamps – one at the top of Portway, one at Badcox and the other eight between the top of Bath Street and the bottom of North Parade. There will also be 263 eighty candle power Nernst lamps, which is 17 more than the original scheme. The erection of the generating station, adjoining Victoria Baths, has been entrusted to Messrs Hodder & Son of Frome.*

So the lamps of Frome were converted and given their distinctive *art nouveau* leaf pattern tops which are beloved by many Frome residents. They were originally painted in a very dark bronze green colour and must have looked very handsome when first erected and illuminated.

There are between 70 and 80 Cockey lamps left, some of which are listed but they still disappear! Does it matter that they are a collaboration of Cockey columns and Singer tops? Of course not! They are still known affectionately as Frome's unique Cockey Lamps!

Notes on the History of Beckington Abbey
by Michael McGarvie

A writer in the *Frome Almanack* for 1925 says of the Abbey: 'little or nothing definite is known about it.' What is known is largely taken from the highly coloured sale particulars of 1910 composed under the aegis of the then owner, Mrs Hume Nisbit. These are entirely erroneous and misinformed and invent a pseudo-history for the building. The Abbey is a large and handsome structure which contains remarkable plaster work so it is understandable that the owners, past and present, should seek a history to match.

History

This house was not an abbey, however, its history before 1641 is obscure. The layout of the buildings and the fact that it had formerly outside galleries suggests that it began life as a great inn of the courtyard type. Such an inn, called the Harp, existed in Beckington and belonged to Terumber's Chantry, a charitable foundation in Trowbridge. It may have incorporated 'the almeshouse of Bekington' mentioned in the will of Robert Parnell in 1502 when he left the 'almes folkes a blankett.' This latter passed into the hands of the wealthy clothier, Alexander Langford. The Harp is recorded as late as 1582.

From an architectural point of view, the abbey has 15th century origins although the earliest datable architectural features appear to be mid-16th century: roofs, window mouldings and archways. There was a great remodelling in the early 17th century when the great parlour with its magnificent plaster ceiling, called by Sir Nicholas Pevsner, 'the most sumptuous in Somerset', was created. It seems likely that by this time the abbey had come into the possession of the Webb family, immensely wealthy clothiers and Lords of the Manor. Robert Webb died in 1641, so if the Abbey was indeed his house, would have been responsible for the fine plaster ceilings and other improvements. It is possible that Webb's widow, Elizabeth, sold the Abbey to James Hayes, a Frome clothier, resident in Frome early in 1641, but of Beckington when his daughter married later in the year. Hayes died in 1662 and his son, Sir James Hayes, leased his 'mansion or manor house with the barnes, stables and outhouses, yards, backsides, gardens, orchards and paddocks of ground thereto adioyninge' to Robert Rundell, a clothier.

In 1691, Hayes sold the property outright to Rundell for £2000. It is described as 'all that Capitall Messuage or mansion house with the appurtenaunces scituate and beinge in Beckington aforesaid with the garden and orchards thereto belonging and one close of meadow or pasture lying on the east side of the said messuage inclosed with a stone wall containing by estimation one acre'.

Rundell died in 1694 leaving his property to his grandson, Samuel Mortimer. He died in 1729 and the Beckington estate was divided amongst his three sons, Nathaniel, John and William. Nathaniel lived at the Abbey for a time; according to Thomas Bunn, his mother, Nathaniel's daughter, was born there. Under a family settlement of 1735, the capital messuage with the workhouses, stables, dyehouse, stove court before the house and three orchards, were allocated to John Mortimer.

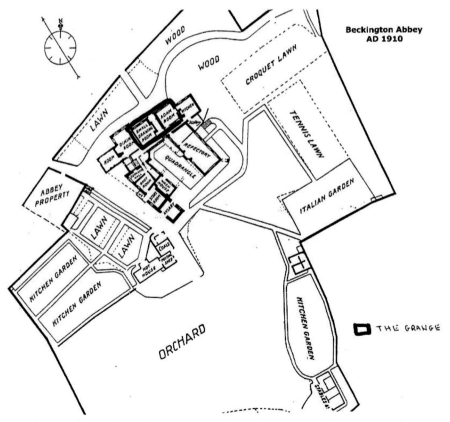

From the Mortimers, the Abbey appears to have passed into the hands of the Hayward family, clothiers. It was occupied by Benjamin Hayward in 1780, then by Mrs Hayward, possibly his widow. By 1803, William Hudden was living at the Abbey and appears to have owned it by 1811. He was still there in 1830 and died in 1837. He was the first to use the building as a school.

The Name

The Abbey is referred to as the manor house in the 17th century but this was spurious as the manorial rights went with Prior's Court Farm. The attempt of the heirs of the Mortimer family to appoint a gamekeeper on the strength of this so-called manor in 1780 was firmly squashed, however, the name 'Manor House' was revived by Hudden's successor, JR Hayward, in 1838. The following year, James Poulter, had a gentleman's boarding school at the Manor House and in 1851, Miss Beck ran the Manor House School. The name was continued by Miss Williams in 1866. By 1872, the Misses Parfitt ran their school from the Abbey House. This led to some confusion with the doctor's house in Goose Street, so the Manor House continued to be used as an alternative. It is the Abbey House on the OS 1886 map but the Manor House in *Kelly's Directory* in 1894. The Name Beckington Abbey appears to have been the creation of Mrs Hume Nisbit in 1907.

NUNNEY.

At Frome Petty Sessions on Thursday—before Mr. R. H. Batten-Pooll, Major A. H. Tucker, Mr. P. E. Le Gros, and Mr. W. B. Lee, Frederick W. Bynoth, posting proprietor, of Frome, was summoned for driving to the public danger at Nunney on Friday, June 12. It was alleged that defendant drove into a crowd of 200 persons who had come for a suffragette meeting, scattering them in all directions; that a woman carrying a child was nearly knocked down; that one of the shafts struck a police sergeant in the back, and that he had to jump with his cycle into the ditch. Defendant said he was driving a blood mare, and something made her jump. The sergeant was in front, and he knew the shaft very nearly struck him, which he was sorry for. He denied driving into the crowd, and said that he kept at the end of the procession. The chairman told him that the balance of the evidence was against him, and he would be fined 10/- and costs.

My thanks to Janet Howard for this extract from the Shepton Mallet Journal, 26 June 1914. Ed

Identification of an old Family Photograph
by Bob Kelley

The notes I received many years ago with my treasured copy of the oldest surviving Kelley family photo stated that it was taken at the wedding at '*St John's Church, Frome in June 1898. In the back-row are Martha and John Kelley, Arthur and Bessie Clifford, Charles Pitman and unknown. Seated from the left are Clarissa Kelley, Lily Harwood, Margaret Kelley and Mrs Harwood. Harry Kelley lies on the grass with the young Edgar Gillingham, who was brought up by George and Clarissa Kelley. After WW1 service in the guards Edgar became a butler in Westbury. He married the housekeeper and later ran the shop/post office in Erlestoke near Devizes.*'

I set out to discover more about the people in this Victorian picture and what happened to them. Given the notes, it seemed a quick and easy enough project, but I immediately hit a snag and it was to take me a year to unravel. If the wedding took place when described, Martha Matilda was still a Frapwell aged 25, as she didn't marry my grandfather John (aged 27) until 13 May 1899.

I could find no trace of the wedding having taken place at St John's. On the contrary, the Parish records of St Lawrence with St James, Clapton on the Hill, Bourton on the Water, (the groom's home) show that the couple's banns were not read there until 18 and 25 June and 2 July 1899.

> No. *202*
>
> Banns of Marriage between *Arthur Edward Clifford, bachelor, of this Parish and Bessie Jane Walton Kelley, spinster, of the Parish of Christ Church, Frome, Som.* were published on the Three Sundays underwritten;
>
> That is to say, On Sunday the *18th June 1899 by W P Williams*
> On Sunday the *25th* ' *W P Williams*
> On Sunday the *2nd July* - *W P Williams*

This was over a year after the alleged wedding in Frome. Other entries confirm that the curate had not simply made a mistake in recording the year, so the couple could not have been married in 1898.

It seemed likely the wedding was in July 1899, soon after the banns had been read, and after Martha Matilda had become a Kelley at Christ Church, Frome on 13 May 1899. The long, dried grass in the foreground tends to confirm that the photo was taken in July or later. John Kelley's formal dress and pride of place beside the couple suggests that, as her older brother, he had taken her down the aisle and given her away in place of their father who had died in 1896.

Martha was 17 in the 1891 census and was listed as a 'wool worker – spinner'. She gave birth to George Rainsford Kelley on St Valentine's Day 1900 and the 1901 census records the three of them living at 30 Butts Hill, a terraced house. My grandfather, John FW Kelley, was an employed coach wheelwright, probably working at the Selwood Carriage Works within 5 minutes walk in Keyford. William Harry Kelley (born in Oct 1903) was always known by his middle name and listed as such in the 1911 census when the family lived at 11 New Buildings, another terraced house, in which my grandfather was to remain for almost 50 years. They had Ivy Margaret (Jan 1907), my father, Arthur Howard (1911) and Harold Jack (July 1915).

My grandfather was 43 when the Great War started and 45 when the conscription of men aged 18-41 began in 1916 and his sons were all too young to serve. Uncle George became old enough just before the end of the war and grandfather too could then have been called up as the upper age limit was raised to 56 in 1918. However, none of my Kelley forebears fought during WW1, although some of our relatives did. It seems the Kelleys stayed at home and simply got on with trying to make a living.

Martha Matilda lived until 1947 (aged 74) and John FW died in 1960 (aged 89) leaving £668.18.2d., divided among his children.

Entries in the *England and Wales, Civil Registration Marriage Index 1837 - 1915* show that Bessie's wedding did indeed take place in Frome in the third quarter of 1899, although it took some time to find her entry as it was mis-listed under 'Kelly'. Another puzzle was why the wedding took place at St John's Church when Bessie was recorded in the banns above as a parishioner of Christchurch. The Frome church records are not yet digitised and are not available online, so I visited the Somerset Family History Centre in Yeovil, which has paper copies. The wedding wasn't at St John's but at Christchurch on 8 July 1899. The notes had the church, month and year wrong, but were otherwise helpful! This means that my grandmother Martha was two months pregnant at the time of this photo. Bride Bessie was shown to be a 25-year-old spinster and her groom was a 35-year-old surveyor. Luckily extra witnesses to the signatures were listed, which helped identify others in the photograph.

The formality of the family's clothes and, indeed, the fact that a professional photograph was taken, is surprising when considering that our family was decidedly working class. The 1891 census shows that Bessie was a dressmaker so perhaps she had made her own dress and those of her two bridesmaids. Tailors, and presumably dressmakers, were notorious for over-estimating the amount of cloth a customer would need to buy to make an item of clothing, ensuring there would be left-over material for their own use. The groom, however, was a professional, so maybe he had hired the formal suits for himself and his soon-to-be in-laws. Moss Bros' formal wear hire department had started in London in 1897.

The bridegroom was the son of his bride's grandmother's sister and brother-in-law, so they were first cousins, once removed. The marriage of cousins is not illegal in the UK, so there was no problem at all with their being wed. The chart shows the relationships.

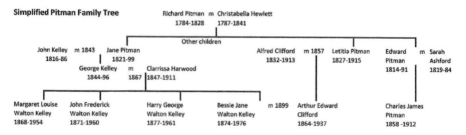

Simplified Pitman Family Tree

Richard Pitman m Christabella Hewlett
1784-1828   1787-1841

Other children

John Kelley m 1843 Jane Pitman
1816-86   1821-99

George Kelley m Clarrissa Harwood
1844-96   1867 1847-1911

Alfred Clifford m 1857 Letitia Pitman
1832-1913   1827-1915

Edward m Sarah
Pitman   Ashford
1814-91   1819-84

Margaret Louise   John Frederick   Harry George   Bessie Jane   m 1899   Arthur Edward   Charles James
Walton Kelley   Walton Kelley   Walton Kelley   Walton Kelley   Clifford   Pitman
1868-1954   1871-1960   1877-1961   1874-1976   1864-1937   1858 -1912

The bridegroom died aged 72 at their home in Nethercote, Bourton on the Water on 15 March 1937 leaving an estate of £5,317.5s. 2d. to his wife and unmarried oldest daughter. He was buried in Bourton three days later. Bessie moved to 43 Broadhurst Gardens, Reigate in Surrey and lived on for almost forty years, until 26 January 1976. She was the oldest survivor of this photo, aged 101¾ years old, and left £2,520.

To the right of the couple is a man identified as Charles Pitman. As the chart shows, my great-great grandfather John Kelley had married Jane Pitman on Boxing Day 1843. Among her several nephews were the bridegroom and Charles James Pitman, who was thus the groom's cousin.

His gravestone is in Spitals cemetery Chesterfield, although his death certificate showed he came from Somerset. I mistakenly believed that in the Victorian era there was less mobility for work purposes than in fact was the case. The Kelleys had remained in the same area of Somerset for two centuries, so what were the reasons behind this migration? West of England towns had boomed since mediaeval times because of the wool industry, whose quality products were sought throughout Europe as the early extinction of wolves in England had allowed flocks of sheep to thrive on the lush grass watered by rains from the Atlantic. However, the Industrial Revolution took the cottage spinning and weaving jobs north to the industrialised mills and the Somerset mines were finding it harder to compete. Rising food prices led to poverty and serious unrest amongst the inhabitants of Frome. In the early 19th century there had been plans to reinvigorate the town, but these mostly failed to be implemented and local economic stagnation caused those who could to look further afield for work.

In 1871 Charles' father, Edward's farm in Podimore was 24 acres, down from 30 acres ten years earlier, so it was not thriving. Charles and his older brother James worked for their father, but such a modest smallholding would have been insufficient to provide a living for Edward, his wife, two growing teenage boys and their younger sister. Probably, Charles left the farm to join the local Somerset and Dorset Railway which ran the main line from Broadstone to Bath. The company failed in 1875 and became jointly-owned by the Midland Railway, which also operated from Bath and had vacancies in Chesterfield.

Charles Pitman's tombstone in Spitals cemetery, Chesterfield states he was born on 3 November 1856, but the 1861 census recorded him as Charlie aged two years old, suggesting a birth date between April 1858 and April 1859 and the 1871 census records his age as twelve. A Charles Pitman is also recorded as being born in the last quarter of 1858 in the Yeovil registration area. He was born on 3 November 1858 and on 20 February 1859 a Charles Pitman was baptised in Milton-Podimore, Somerset. Charles would have been 40 at the time of the photograph and from his position beside the couple; probably he was the Groom's Best Man, despite his less formal suit.

Aged 21, he had married Mary Ann Hopkinson, a machine worker who was 29 on 1 February 1880 in Chesterfield. Their marriage certificate shows his age as 23, so he had claimed to be older than he was to reduce the age difference between them. He would not have been the only man who exaggerated to impress or win a lady, and it was a fiction he maintained to the grave. Just 26 days later their son Fred was born. Charles was recorded as being a 24 year old railway porter in the 1881 census, which also reveals there were 23 Somerset born men, all under 35 years old, working on the railway in Chesterfield. There must have been a strong local drive in Somerset to recruit fit young agricultural labourers and redundant miners.

Clarissa Kelley is seated on the left. She had been born a Harwood from Ilminster and this group photo is of her relations. Clarissa was the bride's mother and my great grandmother then aged 53. She had been born on 3 January 1847 and aged 20 married George Kelley, a carpenter on 24 September 1867 at All Saints Church, Nunney.They lived with her grandmother Margaret Walton at the Theobald Arms, Nunney Catch, where Margaret was reported 'Innkeeper and a toll lessee' in the 1871 census. Following her grandmother's death in 1876, Clarissa and George had taken over the Theobald Arms and the associated tollgate. George had obviously done well, as he is described as 'inn-keeper, carpenter and master of apprentices'. With them were their four children, all of whom had 'Walton' as the third of their given names, and a 17-year-old servant, Sarah Ball.

The Theobald Arms, Nunney Catch

With less turnpike traffic, the family income would have been reduced and there may have been less opportunity for work in Nunney. They left the pub and the 1889 Kelly's Directory lists George as having a shop at 104 The Butts and the 1891 census shows the Kelleys living at 81a The Butts. George is described as a 'Wood pattern maker'.

I do not think that George and Clarissa looked after Edgar Gillingham as it is unlikely that a couple with four adult children would take on such a responsibility without a compelling reason. George died in October 1896, aged 52, before Edgar was two, and I think that is when Clarissa took Edgar in. Margaret may have contributed something to the household from her piece-work earnings as a cloth weaver, but at just 18 Harry would not have been able to pay more than his keep, so it must have been tough for Clarissa to manage without George's earnings. She would have needed another source of income.

Clarissa would have been familiar with the ways in which workhouses operated, as she had lived next to one for most of her life. The Nunney workhouse was next to their pub, and The Butts where Clarissa now lived was a short walk from the Frome Union Workhouse in Weymouth Road. I suspect that Clarissa applied to them for a suitable child to look after so she could receive the 'boarding out allowance' to help towards her living costs. These allowances were paid by the Guardians of workhouse residents as a form of 'care in the community' to free up internal places. Perhaps Frome didn't have anyone suitable, so Edgar was transferred there from Wincanton and put in Clarissa's care. In the 1901 census six year old Edgar Gillingham was described as a boarder living with Clarissa. The 1911 census shows Clarissa living with Margaret, Harry and Edgar at 8 Rosebery Terrace, the Butts, Frome, although her death record three months later reports her to have lived at 10 Orchard St, Frome. She was buried at St John's on 15 July 1911.

The notes say that Lilly Harwood was the younger bridesmaid sitting next to Clarissa. I was sure that Lilly must have been one of Clarissa's nieces and thus the bride's cousin, but I was unable to find her in any of the records of Somerset or its neighbouring counties. Clarissa had three brothers, any one of whom might be Lilly's father. Looking further afield in the 1901 census, I found a Lilly B Harwood aged 15 in Nottingham (daughter of William) and a Lillian B Harwood, aged 17 in Merthyr Tydfil (daughter of Alfred). Due to the distance of both places from Frome, I doubted whether either was the Lillian I was seeking, but I couldn't be sure. The records of Christchurch parish in Yeovil gave Lillian Beatrice Harwood as one of the additional witnesses at the wedding.

The other additional witness to the wedding was Catherine Price Harwood. The 1901 census shows that the Welsh Lillian's parents were Alfred WT Harwood and Catherine P Harwood, however, when I discovered that her father's second name was Walton, it became more probable and confirmed by the entry in the 1891 census for Merthyr Tydfil:

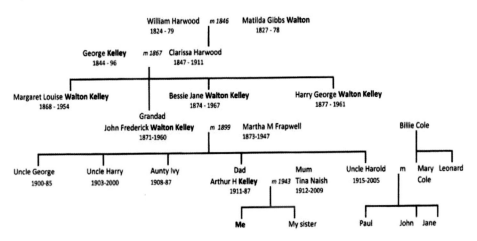

In addition the bottom line shows that Alfred Harwood's niece Margaret L(ouise) W(alton) Kelley aged 22 was staying with them on the census date. She was the bride's sister and 8 years later would be her bridesmaid, as would their 15 year old cousin Lillian. It confirmed beyond doubt that I had correctly identified the two extra witnesses to the marriage.

Lillian's 26-year-old mother Catherine had married 25 year old Alfred Walton Trevelyan Harwood at the end of 1876 in Merthyr Tydfil, Glamorganshire, where he was an engine fitter in the steelworks. He was a blacksmith with metalworking skills and had gone to Wales for work opportunities following the economic troubles in Somerset. Lillian went on to marry Rev Lewis John Davies in Merthyr on 12 June 1909.

I believe that 39-year-old Catherine Price Harwood, the other extra witness to the marriage, is the lady standing beside the best man. Her slim, shapely figure after three children is either due to her petite Welsh build or a triumph of Victorian corsetry. I think she escorted her teenage daughter to Frome, leaving her husband and sons in Merthyr Tydfil. Had they been there as a family, Alfred would have been the witness and might even have given her away. Alfred may not have been well enough to have attended the wedding as he died two years later in October 1901. Catherine lived until 1923.

The older bridesmaid Margaret Louise Walton Kelley, born in October 1868, had given up cloth weaving and was a butcher's book-keeper, still living with her mother in 1911. She never married and died in Basingstoke in 1954, aged 85. Probate of her £858.5s.8p estate was granted to her youngest brother, Harry, a retired printer in Gravesend.

The notes say that the older lady seated on the right is a Mrs Harwood. I was sure she was Clarissa's mother, Matilda Gibbs Harwood, née Walton, aged 72, as the age would match the image. Matilda had married William Harwood in 1846 aged 19 in the Taunton registration area but there is a record of the death of a woman of that name in the same area in the 3rd quarter of 1878 aged 52. I can't find her in the 1881 census and as hers is an unusual middle name I must accept that she died twenty years before this wedding. As the notes describe her as <u>Mrs</u> Harwood she can't be either of William Harwood's two older sisters as she would either have been <u>Miss</u> or have changed her name on marriage. This lady is most likely to be his sister-in-law and thus the bride's great aunt. William had two younger brothers, Charles who died aged 7 and Alfred Webb Harwood, who married Mary Ann Savidge in the spring of 1857. He died in 1911 and she lived until the age of 80 in 1917. At the time of the wedding photograph she would have been 62, but although the image looks far older, she is the only candidate qualified to be the Mrs Harwood named in the notes. I have reservations about this identification.

Lounging on the grass is my Great Uncle Harry George Walton Kelley. He was a print machine minder at Butler & Tanner who moved to the world's largest magazine publishing house, Harmsworth printing works in Gravesend. In January 1910 Harry married Winifred Mabel Whiting, also from Frome and nine years his junior. She died in 1953 and he died in Sidcup aged 83 in June 1961. He should have served in the Great War, but there are seven Harry Kelleys who did, and I can't be sure which, if any, record refers to him.

In September 1978 my Uncle George, Butler and Tanner's retired Chief Engineer, was on holiday in Newquay with Blanche, his second wife, when he was approached by a lady from Gravesend who asked if he was related to a printer named Harry Kelley, with whom her husband had once worked. It seems the family resemblance was sufficiently striking for the stranger to recognise his features and feel compelled to ask.

This is Uncle George in the 1970s, so Great Uncle Harry must also have looked like this in later life.

I cannot verify the note about Edgar James Gillingham, because the census records after 1911 have not yet been released, however, I did find an alternative story.

Edgar was born with no named father in the Wincanton Workhouse in Shadwell Lane on 13 October 1894 to nineteen year old Elizabeth Annie Gillingham who had been baptised in Barwick, Somerset on 8 August 1875. The workhouse closed in 1930 and became 'Town View' the old peoples' care home in which my grandfather John Kelley would die on 13 May 1960. It was later demolished for a housing development.

The 1911 census states he had been adopted by George's widow Clarissa, while retaining his surname, although this would have been informal because state recognised adoption did not begin until 1926. Aged 16, Edgar was an apprentice printer employed in Butler and Tanner's book printing works, having started in November 1907 aged 13 at 3/6d a week. Clarissa died that summer aged 64, leaving him alone for the second time. Unable to survive on his meagre wage he abandoned his indentures on 8 September 1911 and I believe that he then joined the army to be housed, clothed and fed.

I failed to find his WW1 service record, but he must have joined up early, as he was awarded the 1914 Star, serving as a driver in 1st Battalion Training Royal Engineers. As my findings conflicted with the note that he served in the Guards, I asked the Royal Engineers' museum what their files showed, hoping to find his personal data and whom he had named as his next of kin. They told me *'The 1st Battalion training Battalion was based at Chatham, renamed as a Depot and Reserve Formation. If you can't find the service record, that probably means it was destroyed in the Second World War.'* The War Office warehouse (the Army Records Centre) in Arnside Street, Walworth, South East London was hit by a German incendiary bomb on the night of 7/8 September 1940 and over 80% of the 6½ million WW1 records stored there were lost. When the war ended Edgar was awarded the British War Medal and Victory Medal. Men were entitled to a maximum of three of the five WW1 medals when these were issued from 1920.

The notes say that Edgar *'became a butler in Westbury, married the housekeeper and later ran the shop/post office in Erlestoke'* and there is a record of his marriage to Sarah Pledger in Westbury in the first quarter of 1919. Erlestoke is a hamlet six miles east of Westbury, and the 1927 Kelly's Directory for Wiltshire showed Edgar to be a baker at the shop of the Erlestoke postmaster, Albert William Fox, who was also the parish clerk. I found no other record of his wife but an Edgar James Gillingham married 38-year-old Ivy Muriel Edith Mace in July 1944 in Berkshire and they lived at 300 London Road, Reading. Edgar would have been almost 49 at the time of this second marriage. As a baker he may have gone to work at Huntley and Palmers biscuit factory there. He died in Reading on 15 September 1956, aged almost 62, leaving his estate of £5,783.12s.8d to his widow Ivy, so he probably had no children by either wife and I have not found any records to refute this. Ivy died in Scarborough aged 61 in the summer of 1967.

In summary, I believe the oldest surviving Kelley family photograph shows:

Standing (left to right): Martha Matilda Kelley née Frapwell (26), her husband John Frederick Walton Kelley (28), the bride's brother, who probably gave her away, the bridegroom Arthur Edward Cifford (35), his bride/'cousin' Bessie Jane Walton Kelley (26), the best man and bridegroom's cousin Charles Pitman (40) and Catherine Price Harwood (39), the bride's aunt by marriage, extra witness of the marriage and mother of the younger bridesmaid.

Seated (left to right): The bride's mother, Clarissa Kelley, née Harwood (52), the bridesmaid Lillian Beatrice Harwood (15), the bride's cousin and another extra witness, the bridesmaid and bride's sister Margaret Louise Walton Kelley (30) and, probably, Mrs Mary Ann Harwood (62), great aunt of the bride.

On the grass: The bride's brother Harry George Walton Kelley (28) and Edgar James Gillingham (4), Clarissa's adopted son.